GARDENS OF
IRELAND

GARDENS OF
IRELAND

MARIANNE HERON

PHOTOGRAPHY BY
STEVEN WOOSTER

COLLINS & BROWN

First published in Great Britain in 1999
by Collins and Brown Limited, London House, Great Eastern Wharf, Parkgate
Road, London SW11 4NQ

Distributed in the United States and Canada by Sterling Publishing Co.
387 Park Avenue South, New York, NY 10016, USA

1 3 5 7 9 8 6 4 2

A CIP record for this book is available from the British Library.

ISBN 1 85585 713 8 (hardback edition)

A BERRY BOOK conceived, edited and designed by Susan Berry for Collins and
Brown Limited.

Editor Amanda Lebentz
Designer Claudine Meissner
Reproduction by Grafiscan in Italy
Produced by Imago, Hong Kong

CONTENTS

*OPPOSITE The view from the Mussenden Temple,
Downhill Castle.*

INTRODUCTION

Ireland is a gardeners' paradise. The temperate climate, mild and damp all year round, allows a wider range of plants to be grown than anywhere else at the same latitude. The warming effect of the Gulf Stream also casts a 10-mile frost-free band around the coastline where, given shelter, sub-tropical plants flourish. And the countryside itself, with abundant streams, rivers and lakes and constantly varied scenery, provides perfect settings and backdrops for gardens great and small.

Over the centuries, imaginative gardeners have seen in these favourable conditions the opportunity to create gardens as diverse as they are memorable.

Through turbulent periods of Irish history, such as the Cromwellian and Williamite wars and cataclysmic Great Famine in the mid-1800s, and during the golden era of building in the 18th and early 19th centuries, different gardening traditions have taken root happily.

Plants from five different continents thrive in Ireland's gardens today and a renewed enthusiasm for gardening has produced the equally happy offshoot of an increasing number of gardens being opened to the public – there are now well over 100 throughout the country that welcome visitors. Many are privately owned and the owners are often on hand to share their enthusiasm.

ABOVE Zantedeschias surround a majestic bird at Kilmokea.
RIGHT The brilliant show of the yellow spathes and glossy leaves
of skunk cabbage (Lysichiton americanus) *at Mount Usher.*

WHEAT AND EVEN grapes ripen in the sunny south east, in rich land that attracted first Viking and then Norman invaders. The Vikings gave their names to the coastal ports of Wicklow, Arklow and Waterford, the Normans founded walled towns at Wexford, New Ross and Dublin, and, later, the Cistercians came from France to found the great monasteries like Jerpoint.

Gently rolling land is transected by the placid river systems of the Blackwater, the Slaney, the Nore, the Suir and the Barrow,

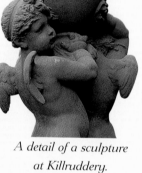

A detail of a sculpture at Killruddery.

their wooded valleys providing some wonderfully pleasing scenery. Wicklow's hills and mountains abound with glens, swift rivers and lakes, so it comes as no surprise that this part of the country is known as the garden of Ireland.

One of the best known landmarks is the ruined monastic settlement at Glendalough in County Wicklow, which was founded by St Kevin in the 6th century. The remains of this early Christian settlement are surrounded by wild scenery of mountains and lakes.

Other renowned sights include the majestic and imposing Palladian houses of Castletown at Celbridge; and of Russborough in County Wicklow, built in the 18th century in the Palladian style and featuring stucco ceilings by the Lafrancini

Autumn colour in the Robinsonian garden of Mount Usher.

A statue of Juno, bathed in sunlight, at Killruddery.

SOUTH & S. EAST

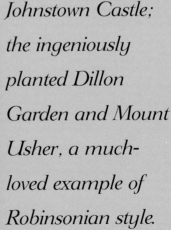

The gardens of the south and south east are wonderfully varied. This particular area of Ireland is singularly rich in gardens of all types large and small, historic and modern: they include Killruddery at Bray, where the 300-year-old Baroque garden remains intact; the Italianate gardens of Powerscourt and Johnstown Castle; the ingeniously planted Dillon Garden and Mount Usher, a much-loved example of Robinsonian style.

brothers. Other attractions are the medieval city of Kilkenny, Lismore Castle and the 17th-century Royal Hospital at Kilmainham, which features a ceiling inspired by what must have been the most awesome of gardens. For those in search of flora, fauna, history and breathtaking scenery, this part of Ireland has much to offer.

The fossil fountain at Powerscourt.

KILFANE

THOMASTOWN, COUNTY KILKENNY

An idyllic glen is the setting for a cottage orné *and dramatic cascade at the heart of an 18th-century demesne in the Romantic manner.*

ROMANTIC IN every sense, this secret gem of Irish gardening history remained lost for over a century and a half. It belongs to that period when, in tandem with the Gothic revival, taste turned from the pretty, pastoral idiom of the Picturesque movement to the embellishment of more dramatic natural features.

In the words of Louisa Beaufort to Sophy Edgeworth in 1819, 'the walk was very pretty, by a stream rushing over large beds of rock, the beeches high and well planted and the ground blue with harebells, the cottage is prettyish – somewhat of a has-been but stands on a tiny lawn near a stream and opposite to a cataract which rushes down the opposite rock'.

Sham ruins, gloomy ravines, raging cataracts and overtly sinister landscapes all appealed to a melancholy turn of 'Gothick' imagination. And in the enclosed, steep-sided glen on the edge of his demesne at Kilfane, Sir John Power found the perfect setting for his rustic idyll in the Romantic style.

A man of great sensibility, Sir John embellished his Eden during the 1790s. The main features were a charming thatched *cottage orné*, facing a dramatic waterfall, fed by water diverted by canal from a river nearly a mile away and a hermit's grotto at the foot of the ravine. Ornamental planting of laurels, rhododendron and ferns and details like benches and bridges

LEFT Once the scene of fêtes and dalliance the restored cottage orné *faces the shimmering curtain of the waterfall (overleaf).*

RIGHT A chair of coppiced wood reinforces the theme of a rustic idyll.

would also have been introduced. Designed to prompt contemplation of nature at her most sublime, such romantic retreats were also the setting for courtship, picnic parties and for entertainments. There are very few examples of *cottage ornés* in Ireland: notably the Swiss Cottage, Cahir and Derrymore Lodge near Newry. The Romantic movement inspired by the rustic ideals of Rousseau found few devotees, perhaps because the realities of peasant life it sought to idealise were all too dreadfully apparent.

Nearly two centuries later, when potter Nicholas Mosse and his wife Susan moved to the former gamekeeper's lodge at Kilfane, they began to reclaim 18th-century rides from the jungle of overgrowth. They puzzled over the ruins of a small building beside the pools and cascades in the delightful glen they rediscovered. But the secrets of the lost garden did not come to light until, firstly, sketches of the cottage were found in the Royal Society of Antiquaries and, secondly, when the cataclysmic Hurricane Charlie sent torrents of water coursing down the canal, recreating the 30-foot waterfall overnight.

Now the cottage has been faithfully restored by architect David Sheehan. The waterfall pours in a crystal arc into a pool at the foot of the cliff and beside it is the gloomy outcrop sheltering the hermit's grotto. Rustic bridges have been created, giving vantage points over the stream as it burbles through moss-covered boulders, and walks through the surrounding woods have been laid down. The latter have become the setting for installations of contemporary sculptures such as 'Air Mass', created by American artist James Turrell and 'Rut' by the English sculptor Bill Woodrow. Other features in the demesne include a bluebell-carpeted glade, known evocatively as 'Heaven', a Victorian fern walk and a reopened prospect to Slievenamon mountain.

Mrs Johnson's precipitous ride above the Glen (named after a member of the last family to own Kilfane) was cleared with great risk to life and limb by Nicholas Mosse. Plants like shade-loving dicentra have been planted in naturalistic carpets, the idea being to recreate as closely as possible the original style of planting encouraged in the Glen. Plants used would have been naturally occurring species such as ferns, bluebells, foxgloves and primroses, plus partial shade-loving

ABOVE The waterfall cascading over the lip of the ravine is fed by a mile long canal.

RIGHT A perfect natural foil to the artful cottage, the stream flows through pools and moss-covered boulders on its way to a rustic bridge.

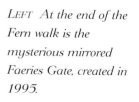

LEFT At the end of the Fern walk is the mysterious mirrored Faeries Gate, created in 1995.

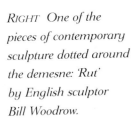

LEFT Mr Butler's Bridge provides a vantage point at the lower end of the glen, to admire the cascading stream and the mysterious Pine Island.

RIGHT One of the pieces of contemporary sculpture dotted around the demesne: 'Rut' by English sculptor Bill Woodrow.

shrubs and plants. The wild areas of the garden are now linked to a series of enclosed gardens surrounding the Mosses' home. There is an orchard, a green haven planted with circles of trees, a tranquil lily pond garden with a loggia for al fresco meals, built with stones salvaged from a former platform at Kilkenny station, and a blue border of delphiniums and lobelias.

The Moon garden, which is planted in silver and white with a circular central bed, comes into its own when pale cosmos and astrantia glimmer in the dusk. The entrance to the walk down to the glen is through the magical fern walk where the vista between towering hedges is completed with the extraordinary mirrored Faeries Gate. This historic demesne is still evolving and there are plans to restore the Hermit's Grotto with help from the Heritage Council; clearance and new planting are ongoing. Seen through the lens of the 20th century, Kilfane seems not so much a folly as a lovely revival of a lost aspect of landscape design.

CAMAS PARK

CASHEL, COUNTY TIPPERARY

*An inspirational young garden where varying
moods and styles meld happily.*

HORSES AND gardens don't usually go together, given the time-consuming nature of both. Thus, counties such as Tipperary (with its traditionally strong equestrian links) have a relatively small concentration of memorable gardens. Camas Park, which is strongly structured and full of changes of mood, is a lovely exception to the rule.

The starting point for this relatively young garden was an old wall. Denuded of self-seeded ash trees, which hid a charming gothic archway, the wall became the excuse for both a secret enclosed garden and the backdrop for deep herbaceous borders and velvety lawns. The sloping site of the garden, which was established less than 10 years ago, was landscaped into pleasing contours and different levels. Through the gothic archway, now enhanced with a decorative wrought-iron gate, is a sheltered courtyard, paved in Liscannor slate and cobbles, which is a haven for tender plants. Golden Irish yews and a pergola covered in double wisteria provide a vertical element and old stone drinking troughs hold collections of alpine treasures.

Lined with trellis, the walls provide a perfect support for clematis and other climbers and such frost-tender plants as *Cytisus battandieri* and *Passiflora caerulea* flourish in their shelter. A circle of beech hedge with a sundial at the centre gives interest to the view from the drawing room window and illustrates just how effective bold, simple features can be. The approach to the

*LEFT A wrought-iron gate
offers a tantalising glimpse
of the secret world of the
enclosed garden.*

*RIGHT Columnar yews,
topiary and terracotta pots
give an Italianate mood to
the courtyard garden.*

house is given a similarly formal treatment. The drive sweeps around beds of white 'Blanche Double de Coubert' roses, which bear showy scarlet hips later in the year; stands of white-stemmed *Betula jacquemontii* and whitebeams underplanted with what the Victorians called a 'laurel lawn'. Nearby, a peaceful sunken garden boasts a graceful bower cloaked in the double, sweetly scented 'Aloha' rose.

A wild water garden concealed in a hollow forms a complete contrast to this formality. A pond surrounded by sheltering trees offers ideal conditions for spring bulbs and for water-loving plants. A circular walk has been created around the pond and through daffodils, hellebores, primroses and magnificent colonies of Candelabra primulas. The area provides the perfect environment for damp-loving foliage plants, ferns, grasses and woodland favourites like foxgloves and anemones. A symphony to spring early in the year, the walk later becomes a quiet green retreat, broken only by the murmuring of doves.

ABOVE An intriguing revival of the Victorian 'laurel lawn' beneath a stand of whitebeams, makes a strong statement.

RIGHT The wild garden is a haven for damp-loving plants such as ferns, primulas and Hemerocallis.

ABOVE Lichens coating old stone troughs harmonise with alstroemerias in the courtyard garden.

LEFT Stone haystack stands mark the entrance to a grassy path between informal herbaceous planting of perennial geraniums, euphorbia and Alchemilla mollis.

KILMOKEA

CAMPILE, COUNTY WEXFORD

*An idyllic compartmentalised demesne
combined with a wild rhododendron
and camellia garden.*

KILMOKEA IS one of those gardens that draw you in, from one pleasing composition to the next, each one more satisfying than the last. There are two contrasting areas: one a series of subtly constructed gardens within a walled garden; the other a secret wonderland with a stream running through its heart.

The first is a lovely exercise in structure, with intimate enclosed areas surrounding the former rectory (constructed in 1794) and the stone dovecote. Each hedged compartment has its own rich complement of detail and offers tantalising vistas of different areas of the garden. The eight acres were created over 50 years by the late David Price and his wife Joan, aided and abetted by their relative Harold Peto. He designed the Italianate garden and 'casita' at Ilnacullin (see page 122) and also inspired the Italian garden at Kilmokea. Here a loggia overlooks a pool where clipped golden privet and a bronze figure are reflected between the water lilies.

The formality of the flagged terrace and topiaried hedges surrounding the pool is offset by self-seeded *Alchemilla mollis*, bride's veil and verbascum. Entrances to areas of the garden create a visual drama all of their own: there is an entrancing gothic, wrought-iron gateway near the 18th-century dovecote and a topiaried peacock perches on clipped yew ramparts above his vivid feathered counterparts. Nearby, a lush pond garden, with its profusion of acanthus, rodgersia and day lilies, has pillars of yew clipped into exotic Moorish shapes guarding its narrow exit. There are more than 16 varieties of

*ABOVE Vivid peacocks
display themselves to their
topiaried counterparts.*

*RIGHT The edges of the lily pond
are softened with plants such as
valerian, alchemilla and dicentra.*

ABOVE The formality of yew topiary offsets the informal planting of shrubs.

LEFT Variegated ivy, box, ferns and wild geraniums frame a classical head.

magnolia, including *M. soulangeana* 'Lennei', *M. grandiflora* and *M. campbellii*.

The wild garden sloping down to the estuary of the River Barrow is planted in the Robinsonian manner with camellias, rhododendrons, azaleas, acers and other exotics sheltered by fir, larch and hemlock, and given definition by winding paths and a spring-fed stream cascading into a series of pools. Over 50 different varieties of camellia flourish in a display of colour that begins in January and is later followed by the blooming of rhododendrons, varying from the deep pink *R. racemosum* to the fragrant russets of shell pink *R.* 'Loderi Venus'. At the head of the natural spring is a mill pond fringed with gunnera and azure blue hydrangeas, where seats invite contemplation of the prospect across the estuary and the swallows that swoop over the water. There is also a green garden, where rivers of hostas, skunk cabbage and rodgersias swirl around a pool.

The garden has taken on a life of its own, casting a spell over new owners Emma and Mark Hewlett and giving them an enchanting focus for their new home and Hidden Ireland guesthouse. Any additions are of the kind the garden itself seemed to ask for: such as a conservatory where visitors can enjoy Emma Hewlett's delicious fare and a pergola planted with old-fashioned roses like 'William Lobb' and 'Baron Girod de l'Ain'. The owners also have plans for the development of the literary garden, a peaceful green enclosed area beside the wild garden with inviting benches for reading and contemplation.

RIGHT A spring display of magnolia, Prunus cerasifera *'Nigra', weigela and honesty frames a small pond garden.*

JOHNSTOWN CASTLE

MURRINTOWN, COUNTY WEXFORD

*Formal gardens, lakes and woodlands
surround a handsome Gothic castle.*

THE GOTHIC fantasy castle and its setting by a lake with views to an eye-catching cascade and ornamental tower represent a perfect marriage between architecture and landscape.

The harmony is deliberate, for both were designed in 1840 by Kilkenny architect Daniel Robertson, who is also associated with the gardens at Powerscourt (see page 42). The inspiration for the heavily turreted castle, built for the Grogan Morgan family around an old tower house, is Norman; however part of the grounds represent Robinson's new ideas on the Italianate style reminiscent of the terraced hillsides and water features in Renaissance gardens. Lawns and stands of exotic timber sweep around the lake, and on the far side

LEFT Swans glide gracefully upon the still waters of the lake.

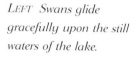

RIGHT A close-up view of the Dolphin fountain – according to legend, dolphins are believed to impart wisdom.

LEFT The Dolphin fountain stands before the porte-cochère, or horse and carriage entrance, to the 1840s castle, which was designed by Daniel Robertson and built from silver-grey ashlar.

BELOW These goddesses are just two of the many classical statues to be admired in the castle grounds.

a broad terrace lined with classical statuary provides a belvedere from which to admire the frowning ashlar castle and its silver image reflected in the lake. Below the terrace, a wide cascade, fed by a rill, tumbles down to the water. The formal garden was also laid out in the Italian manner, with an elaborate parterre, a central fountain and a loggia surmounted by a belvedere. Around the grounds Robertson's designs for the grand castellated gateway, the lakeside tower, the grandiose conservatory and the boat house mirror the Gothic architecture of the castle.

The popularity of the Grand Tour, the desire to display classical artefacts imported from Europe, and the introduction of new plants and trees all contributed to the shift away from naturalistic landscapes to more formal settings in Victorian times. In their day, trees such as the *Araucaria araucana* (Monkey puzzle), *Cryptomeria japonica* and *Cupressus macrocarpa* planted at

RIGHT The five-acre lake mirroring the castle was man-made at great expense.

BELOW The tower in the woodland garden looks like an artful Gothic ruin but it is in fact the real thing, and dates back to medieval times.

ABOVE A magnificent specimen of Cedrus atlantica 'Glauca' provides shelter for a pair of swans.

Johnstown would have been great novelties. There is an arboretum near the castle, originally created to show off newly introduced rhododendrons. The woodland garden, surrounding the ancient ruins of the stronghold of the Rathlannons, is planted with choice trees and shrubs including *Cornus kousa*, aspen-leaved beech, azaleas and magnolias among them. The paths around the grounds are an especially lovely place for a stroll in late spring and in autumn when the trees weep gold and scarlet leaves into the lake and the venerable cryptomeria turns bronze. Among other trees and shrubs of interest in the grounds are the fern-leaved beech, *Fagus sylvatica* 'Aspleniifolia' and the ballerina-skirted *Viburnum plicatum tomentosum*.

The name Johnstown derives from a visit by King John in the 13th century. The demesne boasts three lakes, one of which spans five acres and was created great cost, but happily provided local employment for quite some time. The walled garden laid out in 1844 is no longer kept up as it would have been in its productive Victorian heyday, but the central herbaceous borders have been restored and modern plant houses contain the kind of tender or perfumed plants that would once have been grown for the house. Johnstown is also now a centre for TEAGASC, the agricultural research institute.

RAM HOUSE

*A charming cottage-style garden
full of original ideas.*

RAM HOUSE, nestling behind a stone wall and wicket gate, its Georgian fanlight draped in roses and clematis, is reminiscent of a Beatrix Potter illustration. The garden surrounding it more than lives up to first impressions, for it is packed with cottage-style interest and inspiring ideas.

One of those happy gardens that 'just grew' over the years, its two acres are laid out as a series of contrasting areas, where visitors are irresistibly drawn from one to the next. It is hard to believe now, but Lolo and Godfrey Stevens started with nothing more than a patchy lawn and a dismal *Chaemacyparis* tree. The lawn was gradually replaced with informal planting and gravel paths and the tree has become a prop for curtains of *Clematis montana*, which is but one of the 50 varieties of clematis that can be seen growing through trees or intertwined with old roses.

Like a Russian doll, each little garden contains miniature gardens within it. Inside the gravelled courtyard garden with its banks of old roses and carpets of clove-scented dianthus, there is a secret, shady garden, known as the Piggery, as well as a pool garden and a terrace garden with inviting seating. Another Beatrix Potter touch is provided by statues of animals, which have been dotted about the garden just as though they were in their natural habitats, with a Mrs Jemima Puddle Duck here, a Pigling Bland there and a Jeremy Fisher there. A pergola walk links the upper garden with two green gardens dominated by the soothing

*RIGHT A mellow brick arch frames drifts
of Welsh poppies, cistus and old roses in
the courtyard garden.*

*RIGHT Cottage garden
plants like aquilegia and
santolina spread with gay
abandon in the sunny
south-facing front garden.*

ABOVE A miniature stream cascades from pool to pool in the dappled shade of the wild garden, surrounded by damp-loving plants such as ajugas, Lobelia cardinalis and Himalayan primulas.

LEFT This is a garden where happy plants are allowed to do their own thing: here, white saxifrage carpets a grove of silver birch.

presence of a weeping willow with *Clematis* 'Ramona' growing through its fronds. Beyond them are the wilder parts of the garden where a stream cascades from pool to pool in the shade of a grove of silver birches, its banks lined with water-loving plants and a host of Candelabra primulas.

Each area of the garden is like a separate room, where archways, trees and hedging are used as screens – allowing only a tantalising glimpse of the next compartment. Paths that wind mysteriously around the various features and carefully concealed boundaries make the garden seem much larger than it really is. In the best cottage-garden tradition, Lolo Stevens has mixed old-fashioned favourites like aquilegias, forget-me-nots, white honesty and Canterbury bells with more unusual plants and familiar shrubs: lilac and cistus alternate with unusual acers and shrub roses. Island plantings of roses and shrubs, intertwined with clematis and with carpets of perennials at their feet, form interesting colour combinations and the woodland area glimmers with pale flowers.

Local materials and plants are used in original ways: a variegated ivy forms the edging of a lawn; railway sleepers are used as steps; slate set edge-up in gravel creates a starburst pattern. Plants are placed where they will be happy and then allowed to do their own thing. Ajugas, saxifrage, geraniums, lamium and dianthus form carpets, and southern hemisphere plants like osteospermums and helichrysum bask in sunny corners. The planting, which looks deceptively simple, is in fact, multi-layered, giving a wonderful display from spring through to the end of August. Just to add to the perfection, Lolo Stevens is justly famous for her irresistible homemade cakes.

LODGE PARK

STRAFFAN, COUNTY KILDARE

*A fine compartmentalised garden, filled with
wonderful herbaceous plants within the secret world
of an old walled garden.*

*ABOVE A froth of
Alchemilla mollis edges a
brick path in the potager.*

WALLED GARDENS were once the hub of the self-sufficient world of great houses, providing fruit, vegetables and flowers all year round. A testament to the skill of head gardeners, they were full of vicarious pleasures: buttonholes to be plucked from flower borders; grapes to be savoured in the greenhouse. Now, survivors have become mostly redundant as the need to support large households in this manner has passed.

The two-and-a-half-acre walled garden at Lodge Park, with its deep herbaceous borders in heady tapestries of colour and texture, meticulously clipped topiary, orderly rows of vegetables and espaliered fruit, is a fabulous exception. Features that plant themselves in the visual memory include a small white garden luminous with phlox, agapanthus, 'cup and saucer' campanulas, cosmos, *Lysimachia ephemerum* and silver celmisias grouped around an old stone well head. Equally memorable is a wrought-iron rosarie made by Brendan Walshe and crowned and skirted with old roses like 'Maiden's Blush', 'Henri Martin' and 'Rambling Rector'. These are interlaced with the rich mauves and indigoes of *Clematis* 'Mrs Cholmondeley', *C.* 'Polish Spirit' and *C. durandii*. It wasn't always so. The garden had degenerated and half of it had been used as a paddock, so the present design is a reinterpretation carried out by two generations, in keeping with the late 18th-century Palladian house.

At its peak in June and July, the garden is laid out as a series of contrasting 'rooms' walled in beech hedges. At the heart of the garden is a potager, with serried

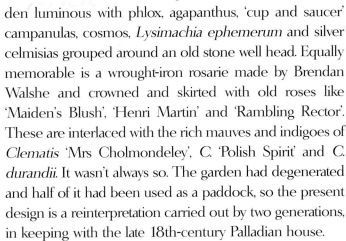

*LEFT A wrought-iron gate in
the beech hedge frames a
view of the herbaceous border.*

*FAR LEFT An attractive
former stone sundial is the
centrepiece of the potager.*

ranks of salads and herbs around a sundial, and flanked by a scented sweet pea walk and cordons of apples on weathered rails. The planting in this lovely garden, seen at its most rewarding in the magnificent border beside the tennis court – where cardoons, *Macleaya cordata* and giant alliums lord it over the penstemons and aniseed-scented agastache – is constantly being revised by the owner, who is a passionate collector of herbaceous plants, and also by gardener Patrick Ardiff.

The classical brick greenhouse, constructed soon after the house was built and fronted by a pool garden and grotto, has just been restored complete with its original water pump. Tender plants like datura, plumbago and tibouchina luxuriate inside. Lodge Park makes a most rewarding visit not only for the perfumed nostalgia of the garden but for the associated Steam Museum and for the delicious cakes and drinks in the Steaming Kettle tea room.

BELOW A memorable composition of white and silver-leaved plants, including agapanthus, Japanese anemones, astilbes and penstemons, surrounds an old well head.

RIGHT *Enviable collections of herbaceous plants are combined in intriguing colour combinations. Here, blue, purple and yellow predominate in plantings of helenium, lupins and argyranthemums.*

ABOVE *Statuesque cardoons dominate the herbaceous border.*

MOUNT USHER

ASHFORD, COUNTY WICKLOW

*Ireland's foremost wild garden with an outstanding
collection of trees and shrubs.*

WILLIAM ROBINSON, author of *The Wild Garden* (1870) described
Mount Usher as 'a charming example of the gardens that might
be made in river valleys … the eye wanders from the Torch lilies
and the gladioli to the blue agapanthus and then to the pine and fir clad roses.'
Mount Usher is one of the loveliest examples of a wild garden in the style
advocated by Robinson: an approach to gardening that suits the Irish countryside, climate and temperament so well.

A glorious stretch of the River Vartry, tumbling over a series of weirs and
crossed by two graceful suspension bridges, provides the garden with a series
of unforgettable vistas. A veritable garden of Eden is laid out on the river
banks, with trees and shrubs from all over the world growing together in the
most natural way amid meadows of naturalised flowers. One of the great pleasures of this garden is in the constant shift of mood and scale. An intimate herbaceous garden walled in beech hedges opens onto a view of the river where acers,
the fossil tree *Metasequoia glyptostroboides*, *Liquidambar* and other unusual
trees create a symphony of spring and autumn colour. Winding paths lined with
rhododendrons, flowering cherries and other choice shrubs give way to a stream
garden – its banks brilliant with primulas, skunk cabbage and astilbes. Woodland
glades carpeted with spring-flowering trilliums, hellebores and erythroniums lead
to the Azalea Walk, which becomes a spectacular perfumed tapestry of coral,
gold, white and magenta in May and June.

Some of the trees in the garden are
stars in their own right, such as a giant
Magnolia campbellii, its flamingo pink
early spring flowers beckoning visitors

*RIGHT Robinsonian-style planting, where shrubs
grow randomly amid naturalised flowers.*

*FAR RIGHT The colourful tapestry of the Azalea
Walk is one of the great glories of Mount Usher.*

ABOVE The graceful suspension bridge affords a magical vista of the river.

LEFT Massed hostas, astilbes and primulas on the stream garden banks.

into the garden, a tulip tree of heroic proportions and a feathery Montezuma pine with naturalised lilies at its feet. This is also a garden for plant enthusiasts, and more than 5,000 species of trees and shrubs are represented, among them notable collections of the southern hemisphere trees, nothofagus, eucryphia and eucalyptus. Over 40 different varieties of the latter alone are represented in the garden and the tallest varieties – *E. viminalis* and *E. urnigera* from Tasmania – are planted as an aromatic grove in the arboretum.

The garden is a true dendrologists' paradise and among the finest specimens are the Chinese fir (*Cunninghamia lanceolota*), the Taiwan spruce (*Picea morrisonicola*) which bears violet cones, *Chamaecyparis lawsoniana* 'Kilmacurragh' and the camellia-like shrub *Franklinia alatamaha* from Georgia, America, which are now extinct in the wild. The garden is cared for by Kew-trained head gardener John Anderson. Aside from giving pleasure, the garden has an important scientific

BELOW The gardens are planted like a veritable Eden on the banks of the River Vartry.

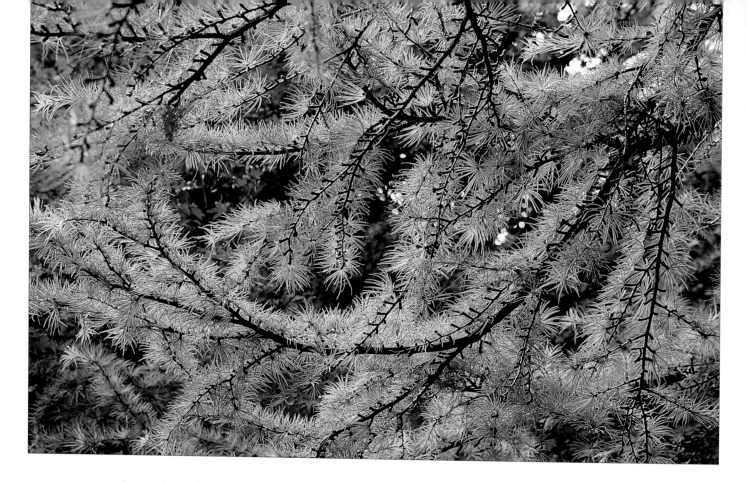

purpose. New plants found in the far corners of the world are introduced here and endangered species are propagated and sent to other botanical collections. The garden was created over three generations after Edward Walpole bought an old mill with an acre of land in 1870 and later left it to his three sons, Edward, George and Thomas Walpole. The family had the advantage of gardening at a time when enthusiasm for newly introduced species, especially rhododendrons, was at its height, and there are now over 150 different varieties of rhododendron.

Horace Walpole continued the gardening tradition and in 1980 Mount Usher was sold by his son Robert to Madeline Jay. Mrs Jay has since become a passionate gardening enthusiast, so Mount Usher remains a happy example of the durability and charm of gardening on the wild side.

*ABOVE The dramatic cinnamon colouring in autumn of golden larch (*Pseudolarix amabilis*).*

FAR RIGHT Betula lutea and Acer japonicum *'Aconitifolium' provide beautiful autumnal colour.*

RIGHT Pampas grass seen against a backdrop of Discanthus cercidifolius *and* Nyssa sylvatica.

POWERSCOURT

ENNISKERRY, COUNTY WICKLOW

*Impressive formal gardens in the Italianate
manner with an incomparable setting.*

THE GARDENS at Powerscourt are on a truly grand scale. A series of descending terraces spectacularly link the Palladian house with a fountained lake and the breathtaking backdrop of the volcanic cone of the Sugar Loaf mountain to give one of the most memorable views in Ireland.

The design is in the 19th-century Italianate manner: the broad terrace is embellished with statues and with a grotto inspired by the Villa Butera near Palmero. A central perron, in a sun and stars design, executed in black and white pebbles, adds to the drama of the composition. From this belvedere the eye is drawn to jewel-like parterres, to a pair of gilded winged horses and to a triton jetting water high over the lake.

The history of the estate stretches back 250 years, but it owes much of its final appearance to Mervyn Edward Wingfield, 7th Viscount Powerscourt. He believed that the planting of trees and shrubs was one of life's greatest pleasures. He planted 10,000 trees a year for 10 years and made his exquisite mark on the Wicklow landscape.

The gardens were first laid out to complement the grand Palladian mansion designed for Richard Wingfield by Richard Castle, which was completed in 1740. In the best Irish tradition, the house incorporated the shell of a medieval castle originally built for the Anglo-Norman de la Poer family. Castle's design for the garden, which included the terraces, rides, the walled

*ABOVE A statue – one of
the many brought back
from Europe – presides
over the lily-filled water.*

*RIGHT The triton fountain
and gilded winged horses
with the Sugar Loaf as a
dramatic backdrop.*

LEFT Flower-filled parterres are set jewel-like in terraced lawns.

RIGHT The 'Spitting Men', bought in Paris in 1872, flank a sundial with the inscription 'I only mark the sunny hours'.

BELOW The central perron, executed in local granite and pebbles.

garden and the round pond were redesigned by architect Daniel Robertson, (first proponent of the Italianate style in Ireland) for the 6th Viscount Powerscourt. Robertson was a martyr to gout and directed the 100-strong workforce from a wheel barrow, inspirational bottle of sherry in hand. Only the terrace nearest to the house was completed at this time due to the unfortunate death of the 6th Viscount while visiting Italy in search of classical statuary for his gardens.

A quarter of a century later, the 7th Viscount used a combination of Robertson's ideas and those of contemporary landscapers to complete the design. Both the 6th and 7th Viscounts travelled far and wide in their search for artefacts: the Dolphin fountain to adorn the former fish pond was found in Paris and the bronze cupids on the lower terrace came from St Petersburg.

If originals could not be purchased, then copies were made. The triton is a replica of the fountain in the Piazza Barberini, Rome, and the bronze urns on the Perron are copied from Versailles. The recently restored winged horses

ABOVE A detail of the curious 18th-century grotto of fossilized spaghnum moss with a shuttlecock fern.

RIGHT The grotto frames a Chinese fortune palm in the Japanese garden.

were specially commissioned and made in Berlin by Professor Hugo Hagen in 1869 and feature in the Powerscourt coat of arms. The professor also sculpted the marble figures of Victory and Fame. Victory nearly ended up being commandeered by the King of Prussia, but fortunately he changed his mind and had a bronze figure made instead.

The 7th Viscount was able to take advantage of the wealth of botanical specimens that became available in the Victorian era, such as the *Cryptomeria japonica* by the Dolphin pool, *Araucaria araucana*, planted as an avenue in 1870 and *Abies nordmanniana* (1867) in his planting schemes. Among specimens of special interest are the native strawberry tree *(Arbutus unedo)*, the black mulberry *(Morus nigra)* and *Picea likiangensis* with its brilliant red cones.

Subsequent generations added new features to the garden. The Pepperpot tower was literally inspired by the 8th Viscount's pepper pot and built in honour of a visit by the Prince of Wales in 1911. A Japanese garden laid out in 1908 features acers, azaleas and Chinese fortune palms. The walled garden is planted with displays of hybrid tea roses and brilliantly coloured shows of annuals and dahlias in season. More rewarding for plantspeople are the double herbaceous borders, featuring a fine collection of covetable plants including *Geum* 'Borisii', *Euphorbia griffithii* 'Fire Glow' and *Geranium wallichianum*. Other features in this extensive garden are the largest pets' cemetery in Ireland, the wonderfully ornate Bamberg gate (1770) which came from Bamberg Cathedral, Bavaria, and a memorial to Julia, 7th Viscountess Powerscourt, with busts of Italian artists Leonardo da Vinci, Michelangelo, Raphael and Cellini.

The Powerscourt estate was bought by the Slazenger family but the Wingfields and Slazengers were united by the marriage of the Slazenger's daughter with the Powerscourt heir. In 1974 tragedy struck and on the eve of opening the house, Powerscourt was gutted by fire. For two decades the great house, which gives the garden its *raison d'être*, remained a ruin. Now the current generation of Slazengers have secured the fabric of the building and have brought it to new life as a restaurant and shop. In the long term there are plans to restore the opulent grand salon to its full glory.

THE DILLON GARDEN

45 SANDFORD ROAD, RANELAGH, DUBLIN

*The best of town gardens created by
Ireland's leading plantswoman.*

*ABOVE A detail of the
Amorini statuette in the
small formal garden.*

*LEFT One of a pair of
sphinxes guarding the
terrace wears a cloak of
Hedera helix 'Buttercup'.*

HELEN AND VAL DILLON'S marvellous town garden is guaranteed to send plant lovers into paroxysms of pure pleasure. So packed with interest and colour that it appears much bigger than one acre, the garden offers that rare combination of being both a collector's garden and a garden which is exquisitely designed and planted.

Since the Dillons moved to Sandford Road nearly 30 years ago, the garden has been constantly revised, as new planting schemes were tried out and yet more delectable plants introduced. The most visually stunning part of the garden in summer are the red and blue borders that face each other across the central lawn. These came about through Helen's desire to rationalise the previous riot of colour. Her answer was simple: to mass all the plants of one colour together, starting with the blues of delphiniums, the blue-greys of nepeta and *Perovskia* 'Blue Spire', indigo *Clematis durandii*, mauve asters and azure *Salvia patens*. Next, all the red plants in the garden were reorganised into a sizzling display where *Penstemon* 'Burgundy', devilish red *Crocosmia* 'Lucifer' and *Dahlia* 'Bishop of Llandaff' vie with the bronze and ruby foliage of *Heuchera* 'Purple Moon' and *Berberis*

*RIGHT Alchemilla mollis softens the formality
of a miniature garden hedged in box and
carpeted with gravel.*

LEFT The pink border in one of a series of garden rooms, ranged around the central lawn. Old-fashioned roses predominate, including 'Souvenir du Docteur Jamain', 'Hermosa', 'Charles de Mills' and 'William Lobb'.

RIGHT Hybrid musk rose 'Cornelia' is used most effectively as a small climber, trained to the arches behind the pool.

thunbergii 'Atropurpurea Nana'. The design of the garden represents Helen's philosophy that plants' likes and dislikes should be paramount. Instead of popping plants into convenient spaces, Helen groups those that require similar conditions, resulting in a garden full of happy and happily cohabiting plants. Helen also likes to use foliage colour to unite colour schemes.

The back of the house looks out over a billiard green lawn lengthened by a forced perspective. A fountain backed by rose arches acts as focal point and a glimpse through a clematis pergola to a distant statue of Diana also increases the sense of perspective. Paths wander through double borders on either side of the lawn and lead to a series of smaller garden 'rooms', each with a lovely complement of plants.

Blue, yellow, orange and variegated plants are offset by an oval of lawn and the dappled shade of an apple tree, and in the sundial garden, small plants from the southern hemisphere like celmisias and agapanthus luxuriate in just the right conditions. Tucked away near the south-facing terrace, where containers are planted with lovely combinations of favoured plants, is a

Victorian-style greenhouse, alpine house and a delectable collection of alpines in old stone troughs.

It seems almost churlish to mention individual plants in a garden so intricately and densely planted that it changes completely several times in a season. From the glorious early display of spring bulbs, such as primulas, hellebores, *Anemone nemerosa* and erythroniums, to the early summer glory of old roses and clematis and through to the full herbaceous chorus, a constantly shifting cast is seen through high summer and early autumn.

However, some plants must rate special mentions for their sheer personality or rarity. These include the hardy purple orchid *Dactylorhiza elata*; showy green-flowered *Veratrum californicum*; a collection of gorgeous antique auriculas like 'Old Irish Blue' with their frosted leaves; new black-flowered *Scabiosa* 'Chile Black'; the tricky giant 'Chatham Island' forget-me-not, which thrives on damp air and seaweed; the very latest *Agapanthus* 'Thunderbird' and lady's slipper orchids like the blushing *Cypripedium reginae*.

One could write a book about the contents of the garden and, in fact, Helen Dillon has written two books: *Garden Artistry* (Gill & Macmillan) and *The Flower Garden* (Conran Octopus), sharing knowledge gathered from decades of experience and field trips as far afield as Patagonia, Nepal and the Andes.

Each year the Dillons undertake one major winter project in the garden. Recently, the front garden of gravel paths and raised rock beds was transformed in favour of a more accessible layout around a terrace of Donegal sandstone, a five-month labour of love that involved moving all the plants.

Only highly favoured plants are allowed a place in this shady, lime-free area. There is a wonderful collection of bulbs and spring-flowering plants, and plants with Irish links, such as the heavenly blue *Meconopsis* 'Slieve Donard', named after the nursery in the Mournes where it was bred, and *Deinanthe caerulea*, introduced by Irish plant hunter, Augustine Henry, who used to live next door.

BELOW The blue border, full of old-fashioned favourites such as delphiniums, goat's rue, larkspur, asters and Campanula lactiflora.

Helen Dillon is a perfectionist – and the garden certainly reflects this. It is also a lovely testimony to two of this talented plantswoman's abiding philosophies. One is that given good structure in garden design, planta-holics can get away with all manner of wild and wilful specimens, which look their best in a strong framework. The other is that plants should look as happy and healthy in a garden as they would in their natural habitat, and that means gracefully accepting that a plant should be placed to suit its needs rather than where there happens to be a gap in the border.

RATHMICHAEL LODGE

RATHMICHAEL, COUNTY DUBLIN

*A flower-filled, cottage-style garden, full of enviable plants,
inspirational planting and old-fashioned roses.*

*LEFT Ivy-collared
greyhounds keep watch
amid perennials.*

*BELOW One of a large
collection of beautiful,
old-fashioned roses.*

*RIGHT The sharp lemon
of* Thalictrum *adds a
spicy note to the
herbaceous border.*

RATHMICHAEL BELONGS to that happy breed of informal garden which positively invites you to wander, glass in hand, to make closer acquaintance with a fascinating assembly of plants. It is, above all, a family garden and an extension of life in the wisteria-clad house. This is a garden that has evolved gently over the years and has become home to a fine collection of herbaceous plants, which have been planted over a 20-year span by Corinne Hewat and are greeted by her like old friends. An old stone wall with a wicket gate leading to an orchard and an exuberant flower-edged vegetable garden bursting over a green picket fence endorse the cottage garden mood.

Visitors are irresistibly drawn to a stunning pair of curved herbaceous borders, their dense planting presenting a shifting colour spectrum, with blues, purples and whites predominating in early summer, spiced with punchy yellows of plants like *Thalictrum flavum*. Later, palest cream buttons of santolina and golden *Inula hookeri* and *Anthemis tinctoria* 'E. C. Buxton' set off some double campanulas, *Veronicastrum virginicum*, phlox, veronicas, helianthemums, the lovely perennial *Geranium pratense* 'Plenum Violaceum' and *Cerinthe major*. Corinne's collection has been gathered from far and wide, with strong, distinctive plants to suit the

LEFT A colourful array
of plants includes
campanulas, alchemilla
and perennial geraniums.

demanding conditions of close planting and assembled in particularly pleasing associations which are constantly reassessed. The owner maintains that the best combinations have occurred by happy accident. The different areas of the garden flow informally into one another with a rose and clematis-covered pergola forming the link between lawns and borders and the vegetable garden.

Old-fashioned roses, both in shrub and climbing forms, are particular favourites in this garden, with blushing, fragrant centifolia, damask and moss roses predominating. Even names like *Rosa* 'Lavender Lassie,' 'Blush Noisette' and 'Golden Wings' are delicious.

The garden is full of amusing touches, like the pair of stone greyhounds wearing collars of ivy. And there are always plans for some new delight. Beyond the tennis pavilion with its cloak of golden hop, Richard Hewat's Millennium walk – an avenue of Turkish hazels *(Corylus colurna)* with views to the granite poll of Katie Gallagher's hill – is taking shape.

RIGHT Useful and
beautiful herbs crowd
behind the picket fence in
the vegetable garden.

FAR RIGHT (from top)
Close-ups of artichoke
Salvia 'Claryssa', and
astrantia.

FAIRFIELD LODGE

MONKSTOWN AVENUE, COUNTY DUBLIN

*A small, inspirational town garden comprising
three contrasting areas.*

A GOLD GARDEN, silver garden and a lush lawn and herbaceous borders could be features of a large demesne. But at Fairfield Lodge they are John Bourke's lovely, small-scale solutions to two pocket handkerchiefs and a room-sized area surrounding a pretty 1780s lodge.

The key to his tiny front garden is structure. In summer, two raised beds overflow with white, blue and silver plants such as *Artemisia* 'Powis Castle', *Hydrangea quercifolia* 'Annabelle', *Malva moschata alba*, and *Crambe cordifolia*. In winter, the shapes of topiaried box come into their own and are echoed by windowboxes filled with trios of box spheres. A back yard has been transformed into a haven, lit with the gold of variegated shrubs, sheltered by a conservatory and soothed by the splashing of a Neptune fountain. Here, foliage is the secret: a pyramid of golden privet; dappled leaves of *Ilex* 'Golden King' and golden hop offset abutilons, cannas, *Clematis tangutica* and showy datura. A classical urn after a design by the poet Alexander Pope amid *Melianthus major* is the focal point of the main garden, while a paved Japanese pool garden known as the 'Bamboozery' provides a change of level. In summer blues, pinks and purples predominate; by June, John's old-fashioned roses are in their stride, among them 'Souvenir de St Germain', 'Gertrude Jekyll' and 'Prince Camille de Rohan'. Sometimes John fantasizes about a garden given over to plants with a small path running through, but that would never do – for where would all the visitors stand?

*LEFT The Neptune
fountain is surrounded by
golden-leaved plants like
Ilex 'Golden King'.*

*RIGHT The Japanese pool
garden, or Bamboozery,
provides a change of level
in the main garden.*

ABOVE Stone spheres, foliage plants and containers flank the steps from the pool garden.

BELOW A detail of the Greek key pattern on the stone spheres.

KILLRUDDERY

BRAY, COUNTY WICKLOW

A fascinating, 300-year-old Baroque garden set against the rugged backdrop of Little Sugar Loaf and Bray Head.

THE GROUNDS at Killruddery are a fabulous example of living history. Beyond the forecourt of the Tudor revival mansion lies a very rare example of a Baroque garden which has survived intact for over three centuries.

The garden has a most entrancing setting, where the rugged backdrop of the Little Sugar Loaf and Bray Head contrasts with the soothing formality of walks, woods and water. The philosophy behind the design is a complete contrast to today's plant-centred approach: order and symmetry were imposed on nature and geometric grounds were seen as an extension of architecture. This was also the era of the garden as a venue for outdoor entertainment on a grand scale: gravity-driven fountains provided theatrical spectacles to marvel at, vistas enthralled

ABOVE The statue of Venus stands dramatically framed in light at the end of the broad walk through the Wilderness.

RIGHT Classical statues, such as this figure of a dying warrior, were used as focal points in the midst of glades or to draw the eye to the end of a vista.

LEFT A pair of Florence Court yews guard the entrance to the walled garden.

Left 'Winter', one of the bronze Victorian statues of the four seasons by Barbezat, which are ranged around the Round Pond.

and classical statuary provoked philosophical thought. The seeds of this great garden were sown in the aftermath of the troubled Cromwellian Protectorate period. Among those who accompanied Charles II into exile in France was the Duke of Ormonde, who was appointed Lord Lieutenant of Ireland following the restoration of the Stuart monarchy in 1660. He returned full of enthusiasm for the style – in everything from fashion to gardening – then in vogue at the court of Louis XIV. Influenced by the designs of Le Nôtre, he had a garden laid out in the French manner at his home at Kilkenny Castle.

The new trend took root among Irish landowners of consequence and in 1682 Captain Edward Brabazon, 4th Earl of Meath, employed one of the oldest tricks in the gardening book and poached a Versailles-trained Frenchman named Bonet away from his English employer, Sir William Petty, to design the grounds at Kilruddery.

Left The lily pond, with its French fountain, is concealed within a circular beech hedge.

Below An imposing statue of winged victory.

Bonet's plan features two long ponds stretching a dramatic 550 feet from the house towards a distant avenue of limes. Known as the *miroirs d'eau*, these canals served the twin purpose of mirroring the house and providing fish for its occupants, and are similar in design to those at the Château de Courance, near Paris. Beyond them are the Cascades, a series of tumbling water features or 'stops', hidden by a ha-ha. The water travels through a half-mile-long aqueduct from its source: a spring in the hills. The Cascades have recently been restored and lead to the Ace of Clubs pond, which is still hidden in the undergrowth.

A curious feature known as the Angles provides further entertainment in the different vistas revealed through walks laid out in a *patte d'oie* (goose-feet) design and hedged in hornbeam, beech and lime. The Sylvan Theatre, with its bay hedge surround and grassy amphitheatre, is unique to Ireland while the Beech Hedge Pond provides a different kind of theatre. Framed in a towering double beech hedge it provides the 'aah factor': hidden inside is a 60-foot circular pond with a French fountain of children at play in the centre. The double hedge provides a mysterious tunnel, green in summer, russet in winter, with windows onto the fountain and Victorian statues of the season by Barbezat.

Beyond stretches the Wilderness, a rectangle of woods transected by shady walks. Filled with the soothing cooing of wood pigeons it discloses a dramatic vista south to a statue of Venus, bathed – Irish weather permitting – in golden sunlight. Bowling was to the 17th century what golf has become to the 20th, ensuring that few towns or houses of note were without a bowling green. Killruddery was no exception – although the green beyond the Angles has now been planted with trees.

The 19th century saw further embellishment to the gardens, with the building of the magnificent conservatory known as the Statue Gallery. Designed by William Burn in 1852 with a dome by William Turner, this tribute to rising Victorian technology is after the style of the Crystal Palace in London.

A charming ornamental dairy, designed by Sir George Hodson, overlooks the two 19th-century parterres, one planted with roses and lavender, the other with low-growing shrubs. A terraced hillside leading to the rocky shoulder of

RIGHT The circular walk inside the double beech hedge is just like an enchanted forest.

BELOW Just as intended, the Miroirs d'Eaux produce a mirror image of the house and sky in their tracts of water.

Bray Head and landscaped parkland, laid out by the 6th Earl, frame the gardens.

It is rare indeed to find a garden which predates its house. All bar a handful of Baroque gardens in Ireland were swept away in the enthusiasm for naturalistic and picturesque landscaping which became the rage in the 18th century. It is also increasingly unusual to find such long-standing owners as the Brabazons, who have been at Killruddery since the lands were granted to Sir William Brabazon in 1618. Long after other fashions of the 17th century – from flowing periwigs and lace to leather corsets and swords – have faded from memory, their garden still remains a place to relive the original sense of wonder.

The soothing formality of the garden, the symmetry of lawns, water and paths act as a foil for the sombre beauty of mature trees. Planted in blocks to create rides, in avenues or used – like the spire-topped Florence Court yews beside the walled garden – almost like living statues, the trees give the grounds a special tranquillity and peace. Among the trees of particular note are the 300-year-old avenue of *Quercus ilex*, a strawberry tree (*Arbutus unedo*) and the incense cedar (*Calocedrus decurrens*). The walled garden was too labour-intensive to be kept up in the old way and is no longer open to the public.

ABOVE The impressive 1852 conservatory designed by William Burn, known as the Statue Gallery.

ABOVE A detail of a border to the tiling in the conservatory, which is home to an exquisite collection of statues.

RIGHT A group of statues in the conservatory reveals exquisite craftsmanship in softly coloured stone.

KNOCKCREE

CARRICKMINES, COUNTY DUBLIN

*A happy combination of a natural rock garden
with a wonderful and varied collection of plants.*

T HE LEGACY of the last Ice Age, which left elephantine rocks exposed through a thin peaty layer of soil at Knockree, might seem a gardener's nightmare. But for Shirley Beatty, who has gardened there for four decades, the natural rock garden presented both a challenge and an opportunity.

The dominant feature of this highly original garden is a massive outcrop of granite – known as *roche moutonée* after a particular form of 18th-century wig! The hollows in its reclining form were transformed into pools fringed with a host of Candelabra primulas which reflect a dark-leaved dwarf acer to reinforce the oriental theme of rock and water. Around the foot of the rock, a wide patchwork of colour, formed by a wonderful collection of herbaceous plants, winds exotically beside a pathway. Each is fascinating, from the delectable *Alstroemeria pulchella* and *Monarda* 'Cambridge Scarlet' to the architectural form of *Rodgersia pinnata* 'Superba' and magenta *Geranium* 'Ann Folkard'.

RIGHT Phormium and a columnar conifer add a structural element to massed planting.

FAR RIGHT A brilliant patchwork of herbaceous plants crowds between granite outcrops and a narrow pathway with Symphytum uplandicum 'Variegatum' in the foreground.

Left Candelabra primulas fringe the pools created in the hollows of giant rocks left by the Ice Age.

LEFT Rhododendrons and shuttlecock ferns flourish in the acid soil of the pine-shaded woodland glade.

These plants and bulbs are woven into fascinating combinations that shift constantly through spring and summer. For a medium-sized garden, Knockcree offers a wonderful sense of adventure. A rocky plateau, where ericas flourish, offers a lovely view of the Dublin and Wicklow mountains and there is a small rhododendron wood carpeted with trilliums and *Geranium macrorrhizum* in season. Other features are a shady garden filled with hostas, hellebores and meconopsis and a more conventional area with lawns, mixed herbaceous and shrub borders, where the house – half hidden in clematis, roses and jasmine – is the backdrop.

Roses, many of them ramblers grown through trees, perennial geraniums and clematis are particular favourites in this garden. The fragrant *grande dames* of the French aristocracy, like 'Madame Caroline Testout' vie with ramblers such as 'Belvedere' (an Irish cultivar), 'Bobbie James' and 'Seagull' and mouthwatering clematis like 'Perle d' Azur', and the violet 'Etoile Violette'.

ABOVE Acer palmatum atropurpureum var. dissectum adds to the Japanese theme of rocks and water.

At every turn there are covetable, unusual plants of the kind not readily found, since many came from friends or were found in overseas nurseries. These include blue-veined *Platycodon albus*, white corydalis and the almost black *Penstemon* 'Raven'. Spring is Mrs Beatty's favourite season in the garden as the first *Anemone nemorosa*, pulmonarias and erythroniums appear. It is an absolutely scrumptious time. But this is a garden which is splendid right through the seasons – visitors come away, heads filled with plants they simply must have.

THE MIDLANDS BOASTS some of the wildest and most unspoilt country-side and has a charm and peace of its own. Away from the main highways, there are unsung areas where there is a sense of having stepped back in time, and where the small-scale features have a pleasing intimacy. Among the many features are the Hill of Slane, where St Patrick lit the paschal fire, the great Stone Age tombs, for example Newgrange, of the Boyne valley, and Lough Kee, Lough Ennell and Lough Derravaragh – lakes hidden in the folds of the impercetible hills.

Central Ireland is rich in remains and and historic buildings: there is Charleville Forest at Tullamore, which is one of the

*Medusa fountainhead
at Butterstream.*

The water garden at Birr Castle on a summer's evening.

Candelabra primulas at Strokestown.

THE CENTRAL AREA

first and finest examples of a castle in the gothic style; the great monastic site of Clonmacnoise on the Shannon; Tullynally, Ireland's largest castellated mansion, and the medieval town of Trim. There are also many fine old houses, and the wide skyline is punctuated by 18th- and 19th-century churches, round towers and tower houses.

Many memorable gardens can be found within easy reach of Dublin, including Larchill, with its many miniature follies, Ballinlough Castle and its glorious reincarnated walled garden; the historic demesne of Birr Castle; Butterstream, which features a compartmentalised garden, and Strokestown, where the walled garden boasts the longest and most splendid herbaceous border in Ireland.

Mask from the Shell Well at Birr Castle.

BIRR CASTLE

BIRR, COUNTY OFFALY

Newly restored historic gardens within a fairytale setting in a 100-acre demesne.

T HE GROUNDS of Birr Castle represent a fascinating insight into centuries of gardening history. An 18th-century landscaped park with a variety of follies, an arboretum with over 3,000 species of trees, a magical, riverside Robinsonian garden and a superb formal garden in the Baroque manner are all represented within the 100-acre demesne.

One of the happiest effects of the gardening renaissance in Ireland has been the restoration of some of the country's great gardens. Birr is deservedly undergoing the biggest restoration scheme of all, in which a large sum of EU funding and sponsorship will be spent on bringing the gardens back to the

RIGHT The terraced River Garden, created by the 6th Earl of Rosse and his wife, lies between the River Camcor and the gothicised castle.

ABOVE Built by the 3rd Earl in the 1840s, the Great Telescope was the largest in the world until 1917.

LEFT The box pyramids and hornbeam arches of the Baroque garden seen through a leafy 'window' in the green cloister.

RIGHT Trained arches of hornbeam form a gothic vault above the walk around the Baroque garden.

BELOW A detail of the Shell Well, one of several follies inthe garden.

glory they enjoyed in the time of Michael Parsons, 6th Earl of Rosse, and his wife Anne Messel. Both passionate gardeners, they enhanced the historic grounds and created the memorable Baroque formal gardens in celebration of their wedding in 1935, and the River Garden on the banks of the Camcor. The centrepiece of the formal garden is an elaborate parterre based on a 17th-century design. It is framed in a green cloister of hornbeam and has entwined 'R's' as the central motif. Beyond these are celestial drifts of colour in the famous delphinium border, planted in a blue, white and yellow theme with particularly pleasing herbaceous plants (some of them hybridised at Birr), like a special Birr hybrid of *Delphinium elata, Romneya coulteri*, and a Birr hybrid of blue-eyed Mary (*Omphaloides cappadocicum*). This area is currently being restored for the millennium.

Many of the rare trees and shrubs in the demesne were grown from seed brought back from the various plant expeditions to Asia and the Americas to which the 6th Earl subscribed, or were propagated at Birr. Best known among them are the gorgeous gold and scarlet-tinged

Paeonia 'Anne Rosse' and the shell pink *Magnolia* 'Michael Rosse'. The history of the Parsons family at Birr stretches back to 1620, when Sir Laurence Parsons acquired the castle and lands. The box hedges, which are more than 200 years old and recorded as the tallest in the world, are survivors from an early formal garden and the parkland in the demesne was laid out around the same time. By the mid-1740s Samuel Chearney was discussing follies for the estate with his patron, Sir Laurence, and the Shell Well was inspired by one of Chearney's designs. In the 18th century, when romantic landscapes, were in vogue, the lake was created and further naturalistic planting added. The Fernery near the extraordinary gravity-driven fountain is a reminder of the Victorian passion for fern collecting. The 5th Earl of Rosse started to plant the arboretum with rare trees from all over the world and created the terraced garden below the castle.

There is a huge amount to see and do in the demesne, where the spring blossom and autumn colours are particularly breathtaking and walks wind langorously around the lake, through wonderful wild flower meadows and around such features as the Ice House and the Winter garden. The gardens of Birr Castle are certainly a splendid horticultural celebration both of the past and of the new millennium.

LEFT AND RIGHT Views of the river walk, showing the contrast between spring and autumn, where a Chinoiserie bridge crosses to an island.

BUTTERSTREAM

*A lovely compartmentalised garden on the flanks of
the medieval town of Trim.*

T HERE IS an unusual picture of Butterstream that made Prince Charles
determined to visit this garden. It shows a cow gazing through a gate
in astonishment at the paradise created from her former pasture. The
man responsible for transforming that buttercup meadow is Jim Reynolds, who
has created the four-acre garden single-handedly over 20 years. His passion
for plants was sparked when, as an archaeology student, he visited Vita
Sackville- West's garden at Sissinghurst. Here was a style of gardening he could
relate to: strongly structured, like a series of rooms, and utterly different from
the typical wild Irish garden. He began to expand the area around his parents'
cottage, swallowing up sections of their farm and embracing the stream that
gives the garden its name.

First came a box *allée* with compartments hiding the spindly legs of such
grand old dames of the rose world as 'Duchesse de Verneuil' and 'Madame de
la Roche Lambert'. Next came a green garden filled with massed hostas,
bergenias and pulmonarias in front of a pineapple-topped folly; then a little hot
garden enclosed by beech hedges where reds, yellows and oranges shock the
senses and, finally, a peaceful streamside garden.

These are grounds that draw you into a world that is enclosed, yet always
offers a tantalising glimpse of an intriguing folly to invite further exploration.
There are some wonderful stories attached to Jim Reynolds' many follies. For
years he hankered after a Tuscan temple reminiscent of Harold Peto's casita
on the magical island of Ilnacullin (see page 122), before spying a derelict
pillared gate lodge. Two years later, Jim bought the ruin at auction and took his
brothers and sisters to dismantle it. After that, inspiration began to take over
and resulted in the gorgeous temple overlooking a lily pool. Liscannor paving
and terracotta pots complete this classical retreat in the heart of the garden.

*RIGHT Precision-clipped box hedges, Liscannor paving
and terracotta pots surround the classical retreat in the heart
of the garden.*

LEFT Echinops and eupatorium make a final display beyond the prim box hedges.

BELOW Sentinels of bay stand guard beside the kale pots in the potager.

Drifts of white willow herb waving beyond precision-clipped box hedges only serve to emphasize the formality. The herbaceous borders at Butterstream reduce visitors to silent wonder as they drift along grass paths running between 25-foot deep ranks of blooms. The planting scheme in this horseshoe-shaped area represents a beautifully controlled exercise in colour associations, with blues and yellows such as lactuca, *Campanula lactiflora*, *Anthemis tinctoria* 'E. C. Buxton', *Eryngium alpinum* 'Slieve Donard' on one side, and deep reds and blues on the other. There are other delights waiting to be discovered: a laburnum tunnel which rains gold in spring; a formal obelisk garden; a kitchen garden; summer houses and a lime *allée* marching off into the distance to claim yet another virgin field. There are also a number of rare Irish cultivars in the garden, like *Bergenia* Ballawley Hybrids and *Primula* Lissadel Hybrids.

Jim Reynolds' latest folly is a pair of new Georgian pavilions for teas and events such as concerts and weddings. For, like all the best gardens, Butterstream will never be finished. So next year there will probably be another addition to Butterstream and a folly that makes perfect sense!

LEFT The Reynolds' Rapunzel tower is half hidden by a glorious display of autumn grasses.

EMO COURT

EMO, COUNTY LAOIS

*A landscaped estate and arboretum provide the
perfect setting for James Gandon's masterpiece.*

THE ORNAMENTAL demesne at Emo remains very much in the early 18th-century tradition, where the landscaped grounds provide the setting for James Gandon's monumental masterpiece.

The story of Emo reflects the strong link between history and the fate of Irish houses and their estates. Emo Court was designed by James Gandon for his patron, John Dawson, 1st Earl of Portarlington, at a time when the phase of great house building was at its height. Emo (the name comes from the Irish Imoe) was begun in 1790 but was not completed until nearly a century later.

The 1st Earl was killed in the 1798 rebellion; the 2nd Earl, although short of money, managed to have the garden front of the house completed by Lewis Vuillamy in the 1830s. In the aftermath of the Great Famine, the estate came near to being sold before the 3rd Earl added the centrepiece of Gandon's design – the rotunda inspired by the Parthenon – and completed the building.

The park at Emo is in the naturalistic landscaped style, with stands of timber, designed to conceal boundaries and create vistas, and with a 20-acre lake – an essential feature of this era of landscape design – in the middle distance behind the house. The magnificent mile-long avenue of Wellingtonias (*Sequoiadendron giganteum*) formed the original approach to the house. These giants from the mountains of California were first introduced in 1853 and were named in honour of the Duke of Wellington, who

*LEFT A series of glades between the house
and lake are planted with azaleas,
rhododendrons and camellias.*

*ABOVE Classical statues were retrieved from
the lake where they were buried by Jesuits
who wanted to hide their pagan nudity.*

ABOVE A magnificent avenue of Wellingtonias lines the original driveway to the house.

had died the previous year. Behind the house is a small formal garden with walks between classical statues and Florence Court yews which originated from the Florence Court estate in County Fermanagh in the 1760s. The ruined Temple gazebo on the estate probably pre-dates the house.

After the last of the Portarlingtons left in the 1920s, Emo became a seminary before being rescued from decline in 1969 by Mr Cholmeley-Harrison, who restored the house and grounds. Grassy rides and vistas were recreated and a wild Robinsonian garden with azaleas and camellias was planted between the lake and house.

Trees were Cholmeley-Harrison's greatest love and, amid wildflower meadows, he created a wonderful new arboretum where fascinating specimens include *Abies forrestii*, with its violet fir cones, and the fascinating handkerchief tree *Davidia involucrata*, discovered by the French missionary Père Armand David in China in 1869.

In a lovely marriage between old and new, a broad grassy ride was created though the arboretum to the focal point of the vista – the Golden Gates. The planting carried out by Cholmeley-Harrison within the framework of existing timber has now matured, and the grounds are especially lovely in late spring

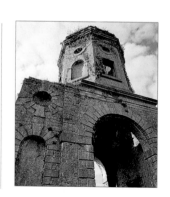

LEFT Trees are the great glory of the splendid ornamental grounds, particularly in autumn

RIGHT The imposing portico of James Gandon's 1790 country masterpiece.

and autumn. Wild flowers, including carpets of bluebells, primroses and milkmaid's smock, provide their own spring display, while shrubs like *Parrotia persica* and *Fothergilla major* turn brilliant shades of vermillion, orange and claret during October.

Grassy walks and paths meander around the estate, including one known as Mad Margaret's Walk, which is named after an unfortunate housemaid who hanged herself from a tree. Emo has now been donated to the nation by its benefactor and is in the care of Dúchas, the Heritage Service. The 35 hectares of grounds and Gandon's spectacular mansion, with its restored interiors and collection of antiques and paintings, make Emo Court a perfect destination for a day's outing.

LEFT The ruined gazebo has an octagonal tower atop a triumphal arch.

RIGHT A classical statue is framed by an avenue of formal yew trees.

LARCHILL

KILCOCK, COUNTY KILDARE

*A rural Arcadia where extraordinary follies and
rare pigs in palaces feature in Ireland's only* ferme
ornée: *a unique survivor of gardening history.*

A PUCK GOAT PLAYING king of the castle on top of a miniature fortress and Saddleback pigs sunning themselves in front of a Gothic porcine palace are the first sights to greet visitors to Larchill. But what might seem to be a flight of eccentricity is, in fact, a unique survivor of Irish gardening history. Had it not been for a happy chance, Europe's only surviving example of a *ferme ornée* might have crumbled, unrecognised, into the pastures of Kildare.

Michael de las Casas and his wife Louisa fled London in 1994 in search of rural peace, and fell in love with the 1740s house at Larchill. But they were unaware of the *raison d'être* for the curious ruins on their 60-acre farm until garden historian Paddy Bowe came to visit and returned from a walk ecstatic about his extraordinary discovery. Here, he declared, was a lost Arcadian garden which simply had to be restored. Four years later, the couple's conviction that they should follow his advice has resulted in the restoration of a two and a half centuries old Elysian vision.

Beyond the farmyard, pasture occupied by rare breeds of sheep and cattle falls gently to the lake with a magnificent panorama across Kildare to the Dublin and Wicklow mountains. But the real eye catcher is the incredible fortress, floating mirage-like on an island in the lake, the scale of its miniature towers and battlements betrayed by an overarching

*LEFT The handsome
Gazebo, which marks the
half-way point on the
lakeside walk, offers
marvellous views back
towards the house.*

*RIGHT The mound under
the Foxes' Earth contains
two tunnels for the fox to
escape from the hounds.*

*ABOVE Mock naval
battles were once staged
around the five-towered
diminutive fortress known
as the Rock of Gibraltar.*

*LEFT A second island
folly is in the shape of a
Greek monopteral temple,
which has a plunge pool
in its centre.*

*RIGHT Unusually, the
Gothic boathouse is dug
into the bank of the lake.*

yew tree. Known as the Rock of Gibraltar, it is just one of a series of follies created in the mid-18th century by an upwardly mobile family of haberdashers. Much visited as 'the most fashionable garden in all Ireland' the estate was embellished by the Prentice family of nearby Phepotstown House during the brief rage for ornamental farms.

Arcadian gardens were part practical working farms, part outdoor entertainment on a grand scale, where visitors could admire rare breeds housed in architectural grandeur and marvel at man-made features ranging from lakes to shell houses. The aim of the gardens, explains Michael de las Casas, was to

RIGHT Rare Berkshire, British Lop and Saddleback pigs are among the occupants of elegant Gothic pigsties.

BELOW A sow looking very much at home in a porcine palace.

create an inward-looking enclosed world where nature was beautified and walks and vistas were enhanced with statuary and poetry was inscribed and garden flowers planted close to seats. What prompted the Prentices to create the *ferme ornée* may have been a desire to keep up with the Wesleys at neighbouring Dangan, the setting for an ambitious 100-acre lake and island fortress (also known as Gibraltar).

What is so beguiling about Larchill is the sheer diversity of the follies. There is a second island crowned with an monopteral temple, containing the 18th-century equivalent of a plunge pool, a *feuillée* (a mound topped by a spiral of trees), a curious subterranean boat house, a lakeside gazebo and a Cockleshell Tower overlooking the newly replanted walled garden.

Most curious of all is the Foxes' Earth, created for Robert Watson who bought the estate after the Prentices went bankrupt. A keen master of the Meath foxhounds, he had the temple-topped mound with its escape tunnels created as a precaution, lest he should be reincarnated as a fox.

In a truly magical way the wheel has turned full circle and visitors are once again flocking to Larchill to marvel at the largest collection of rare breeds in Ireland and at the happy marriage of fantasy and nature.

BALLINLOUGH CASTLE

CLONMELLON, COUNTY WESTMEATH

Splendid walled gardens restored to their Edwardian heyday in a lake and woodland setting.

THIS 17TH-CENTURY castle on a bluff, overlooking a lake in the curve of a wooded hill, conjures up many a fairy tale. The estate contains a landscaped park and a magnificent recreation of an Edwardian garden in three and a half acres of walled gardens. There have been O'Reillys at Ballinlough since the castle was built in the 17th century on the site of a medieval tower house beside a natural spring-fed lake. In 1800, Sir Hugh O'Reilly – who changed the family name in 1812 to inherit under the will of his Nugent uncle – had a canal dug, and built the romantic Rock Bridge across it.

ABOVE AND LEFT A lovely indicator of pure air: lichens shown in close up growing on the sundial (left), which marks the hours of sunshine in the walled garden.

A second lake, linking the existing lake and canal, was dug during the Great Famine (1845) and a turf island was built. The gardens for fruit, flowers and vegetables, with heat-retaining brick-lined walls, were built by Sir Hugh in the 1820s. But the fortunes of the estate declined and a generation ago the castle was narrowly saved from demolition. By the mid-1990s, the walled area had become a ghost garden. Now a splendid transformation has taken place under the Great Gardens of Ireland Restoration Programme, thanks to the enthusiasm of owners John and Pepe Nugent and head gardener Ursula Walsh with design input from Jim Reynolds of Butterstream (see pages 80-83).

A fine double herbaceous border, changing colour from pale pastels in spring to fiery reds and yellows in a late summer

RIGHT Glorious diversity: alchemilla, silvery stachys, perennial geraniums, astrantia and delphiniums are among the favourites used for the double herbaceous borders.

Left *A log cabin hidden*
in the woods is a perfect
trysting spot. It also acts as
a wonderful rustic Wendy
house for children explor-
ing the garden.

finale, forms the central showpiece of the garden. Beech hedges create secluded
compartments within the main garden, while the sunken garden has become
a tranquil pool garden, and a magnolia walk is taking shape. The reincarnated
Rose garden has cruciform paths edged in a haze of *Lavandula stoechas*
'Papillon', backed with informal plantings of shrubs and old-fashioned fragrant
roses. Gothic wooden gates in the walls are copied from Prince Charles' garden at Highgrove; beyond them lies the dappled light of a woodland walk, water
garden and lakeside walks. From the far side of the lake there are rewarding
views of the castle, presiding over its reawakened sleeping beauty of a garden.

ABOVE A moss-
covered fallen chestnut
looks for all the world like
a gothic feature.

RIGHT The rustic bridge is
a romantic feature cross-
ing a sham river.

STROKESTOWN PARK

STROKESTOWN, COUNTY ROSCOMMON

*A handsome re-incarnation of a walled
Edwardian garden, featuring the longest herbaceous
border in Ireland.*

*LEFT An architectual
feature from the original
house acts as a focal point
at the end of the walled
garden beyond the
lily pond.*

*RIGHT Water lilies
(Nymphaea alba) float
in the still water of the
lily pool.*

*ABOVE A nymph reflected
in the water of the lily pool.*

STROKESTOWN IS a lovely example of the Irish gardening renaissance. An Edwardian garden has been reinterpreted within the four-acre walled grounds, with all the glories one might expect of that era of horticultural creativity. It is now more splendid than it would ever have been in the past.

The story of Strokestown Park is an interesting illustration of the rise, fall and resurrection of the 'big house' in Ireland. The original house was built in the late 17th century for the Mahon family on land confiscated from the O'Conor clan. In the 1740s, it was extended in a Palladian design by Richard Castle, who also created an ornamental park and walled gardens. Strokestown is associated with a particularly black episode of Irish history: following evictions of his tenants, Major Denis Mahon was shot during the Famine.

During the last chapter of the Mahons' ownership, Strokestown Park was in decline and was purchased from ailing Olive Hales Pakenham Mahon by her neighbour, Jim Callery. The house and gardens were restored and opened to the public and a Famine Museum created in the stables.

Where a few years ago, there was only a derelict garden, a total transformation has taken place. A glorious 18-foot deep double herbaceous border – quite the longest and grandest in Ireland – stretches down one side of the garden. Planted in the

manner of Gertrude Jekyll, it glows with horizontal drifts of colour, merging from blues, yellows and greens at one end, through hotter shades, to cooler pinks, mauves and silvers at the far end.

    The rest of the garden has a series of beautifully interlinked features and contained vistas, enclosed by beech hedging. There is an Alphabet Walk, inspired by an Edwardian book of alphabet puns, where each area will contain a piece of sculpture depicting a letter of the alphabet; a lily pool backed by an architectural feature; a maze and a green garden filled with ferns and damp-loving plants. The Edwardians – inspired by the new varieties of rose and by

ABOVE The planting in the herbaceous garden is in the manner of Gertrude Jekyll, with colours running from cool to hot. Stately Macleaya cordata *cools the fiery colours of monardas, salvias and alstroemerias.*

ABOVE In the gold section, spires of Lysimachia punctata *and* Ligularia 'The Rocket' *are planted with drifts of* argyranthemums.

books like Gertrude Jekyll's *Roses for English Gardens* (1902) – were great rose enthusiasts. At Strokestown, the rose beds are laid out around a sundial and overlooked from the vantage point of a raised terrace and pergola (another favourite Edwardian device). Other period details, such as a tennis and croquet lawn, have also been retained. The recreated garden was designed by Jim Reynolds, Luke Dodd and Helen Dillon, and executed by garden consultant Rachel Lambe and the then head gardener Catriona White. Combined with a tour of the house and the Famine Museum, a tour of Strokestown makes for a very satisfying visit.

HEDGEROWS lined with scarlet fuchsia and montbretia, lakes and streams fringed with pretty meadow sweet and yellow flags are familiar features of the wild countryside amidst the scenic beacons of Connemara and the Ring of Kerry. There are many other aspects to the south west, such as the bountiful grasslands of the vales, including the Golden Vale and the Mitchelstown Vale, the limestone moonscapes and alpine flora of the Burren in County Clare, the Shannon complex that makes a virtual island of Connaught and the jagged coastlines of West Cork and Kerry, where the rocky toes at the foot of Ireland are warmed by the Gulf Stream.

Willow dragon at Ballymaloe.

The bones of history are laid bare here in the Stone Age settlements at Lough Gur, the early Christian churches and beehive huts in the Dingle Peninsula and Skellig Michael, and the great 13th-century cathedral on the Rock of Cashel. Yet more historic heritage can be found in the Norman towns of Carrick-on-Suir, Clonmel, Roscrea and Youghal, some of which still have their medieval walls. In the past, the south-west

The temple and pool in the island garden of Ilnacullin.

Rhododendrons bloom by the wild shore at Derreen.

THE SOUTH WEST

The gardens of the south west are often crowned by breathtaking settings, such as the island of Ilnacullin, which lies in the wooded arms of Glengarriff, and the lush, sub-tropical Derreen, which contrasts dramatically with the wildness that surrounds it, Annes Grove lies on sheltered slopes above the Awbeg River , Lisselan nestles in a lush and verdant valley and Ballymaloe Cookery Gardens offer a feast for the senses.

coast was more accessible to the flank of Europe for trade, smuggling and the threat of invasion by the French and Spanish, and even today this area feels very remote from the bustle of Dublin. The Dingle Peninsula, known as 'Ryan's Daughter' country, the charming city of Cork on the River Lee, and Blarney Castle with its stone of eloquence – are key attractions on the south-west map.

A flock of hens peck contentedly at Ballymaloe.

ANNES GROVE

CASTLETOWNROCHE, COUNTY CORK

*An extensive wild garden in a beautiful
river valley setting with an old walled
garden at its heart.*

*LEFT Showy bracts of
Cornus kousa glimmer in
the spring sunshine beside
the main walk.*

A CURIOUS 18TH-CENTURY 'mount' in a walled garden, a sheltered glen, jewelled with stands of rare rhododendrons and a lush river garden are the three contrasting areas encompassed by the historic gardens at Annes Grove in the beautiful wooded valley of the Awbeg River.

The brick-walled garden is contemporary with the charming late 18th-century house and is dominated by the mount, an intriguing relic of gardening history. These mounds often had paths or hedges spiralling around them and were devised as vantage points or to give bird's eye views of

*RIGHT The fleshed petals
of Magnolia kobus form
both a canopy and a
carpet underfoot. Purple-
flowered tulips add to the
Spring spectacle.*

LEFT This Kingdon Ward rhododendron introduction in the Robinsonian garden is at the height of its glory in late April.

FAR LEFT A world apart – verdant lysichiton flourishes in the green jungle beside the river.

elaborate parterres. Now the mount overlooks a compartmentalised garden with a double herbaceous border, formal rose beds and a pond garden, which is surrounded by tender shrubs and attractive drifts of white hoheria and eucryphia blossom in summer.

Two generations ago, Richard Grove Annesley, grandfather of the present owners, Patrick and Jane Annesley, spent half a century creating an extensive wild garden in the Robinsonian manner. A keen plantsman, he subscribed to plant collecting expeditions, particularly those of Frank Kingdon Ward to the Far East in the early 1900s.

The sheltered valley provided an ideal site for Richard Annesley's collection of new rhododendron introductions, grown from seed. Their botanical names often recall their origins: yellow-flowered, red-flared *Rhododendron wardii*, named for Ward, *R. yunnanese*, and *R. cinnabarinum* with its waxy red bells from the Himalayas. There are stunning large-leaved rhododendrons with unfurling leaf buds like russet velvet gloves, such as *R. falconeri* with its cream trusses and *R. sinogrande* with its red splotched, ivory-coloured trumpets. Among the magnificent trees and shrubs lining the side of the valley are magnolias, *Cornus chinensis* and *C. alternifolia, Azara microphylla*, thujas, sequoias and cedars.

Below them is an entirely different world, where the river swirls round bamboo-crowned islands and through a host of foliage plants, including gunneras, lysichiton, rodgersia, and winding paths seem like tracks through a mysterious jungle. *Primula florindae*, astilbes and hemerocallis have naturalised on the banks of the river, and watch over the brown trout which dart beneath the rustic bridge.

BALLYMALOE

COOKERY SCHOOL GARDENS, SHANGARRY, COUNTY CORK

*Practical as well as decorative, the gardens at
Kinoith supply Darina Allen's Ballymaloe Cookery
School with delicious produce.*

THE GARDENS AT Darina Allen's Cookery School provide a perfect feast for the senses, where scent, colour and design combine in a glorious recipe. While 'simply delicious' is Darina Allen's catchphrase for food, her approach to the gardens has been to take 'simply the best' from gardening tradition.

Edwardian herbaceous borders with planting coloured in Gertrude Jekyll's palette, an ornamental potager, an 18th-century style shell house, a fruit garden and a herb garden in the 17th-century manner are all represented in the 10-acre grounds. The gardens grew from Darina's conviction that – after food – gardening was to be the next growth industry in the leisure market. To prove the point, the gardens at Kinoith have expanded to claim whole fields of the former fruit farm. Practical as well as decorative, they revive the tradition of self-sufficiency that lay behind the walled gardens of previous centuries: the produce from the gardens supplies the cookery school and restaurants at Ballymaloe.

When Tim and Darina Allen first came to Kinoith, nothing remained of the original 19th-century compartmentalised garden except overgrown beech hedges. This area became the setting for an elaborate box-edged parterre planted with herbs: a peaceful enclosed place, soothed by the symmetry of gravel paths and clipped hedges; the cooing of doves and aromatic scents. Both medicinal and culinary, the herbs are also wonderfully decorative and among the more unusual

LEFT Culinary and medicinal herbs, like this Moroccan mint, each have their own labels for easy identification.

FAR LEFT Living tapestry: the cutwork parterre planted with unusual herbs and sheltered by a venerable beech hedge.

ABOVE An endearing
willow wand scarecrow
complete with straw hat.

ABOVE AND RIGHT Chard
pots and antique cloches
for forcing vegetables.

plants are blue-flowered hyssop, angelica, garlic, chives, variegated horseradish and ginger and apple mint.

Sheltered from wind and marauding hens by a grove of trees, the hidden kitchen garden at Kinoith was inspired by the potager at Villandry, in France. Colourful vegetables are planted in patterns framed in formal brick paths laid out in a diamond design. The carefully organized ranks of lettuce, ruby chard, purslane and purple-black orach are guarded by scarecrows that have been woven from willow wands.

Giant sunflowers, cardoons and Jerusalem artichokes tower over love-in-the-mist, cornflowers, nasturtiums and calendula, which are grown for drying, as garnishes and to ward off pests. A beech house ingeniously created from trained copper beech provides a vantage point from a sheltered seat at the far end of the garden. Here Darina's sister and head gardener Susan Turner, and gardeners Eileen O'Donovan and Haulie Walsh come early each morn-

ABOVE AND RIGHT
Cockles, mussels, scallops
and other Irish native
shells have been used for
the elaborate design for the
interior of the Shell House.

ing to gather herbs, garnishes and other produce for the now famous restaurant and cookery school.

Stretching out gloriously to frame a vista of the Shell House, the new double herbaceous border provides a tremendous tingle factor. Planted in colours ranging from cool through to hot, five-metre deep borders are at their stunning best in July and August. Old favourites like phlox, heleniums, campanulas and delphiniums are combined with newer introductions like *Stipa gigantea* and new varieties of penstemons, agapanthus and salvias, forming a fitting prelude for the climax of the Shell House. From the outside, the simple hexagonal grotto gives no clue to the enchanting decorative wonders within.

Shell houses were often a feature of 18th-century ornamental demesnes – like those at the great Irish houses Carton, Curraghmore and Tullynally. Completed for Darina and Tim's wedding anniversary and incorporating family initials, Welsh shell artist Blot Kerr Wilson took four months to complete the intricate designs of cockle, mussel, scallop and other native shells, all collected by Darina.

Spring clothes the ornamental fruit gardens in blossom, with hellebores, primroses and spring bulbs adding to the display. In summer, clematis like violet 'Pamela Jackman' wreathe among the fruit as it ripens on espaliers and arches. Among old favourites, like 'Beauty of Bath' and 'Lane's Prince Albert' apples, are some curiosities such as jostaberries and a nashe (which is a cross between a pear and an apple), a mulberr tree, an almond and even an olive tree.

Beyond the water garden, where a willow-crafted dragon greets visitors to the new garden shop and café, stretches the beguiling vista of Ballycotton Bay and Knockadoon Head. Seagulls fly in for a bird's eye view of the changing garden: a Celtic yew maze, designed by Peter Lamb, was planted in 1997; a temple will soon be completed and a Memory garden is currently under way. There seems to be no end to the delectable treats, both horticultural and culinar, in store at Ballymaloe.

DERREEN

KENMARE, COUNTY KERRY

*An exotic, subtropical Robinsonian garden set
against a backdrop of rugged mountain scenery
on a wild Kerry peninsula.*

WHERE THE KERRY coastline pokes long fingers into the warming Gulf Stream, Lord Lansdowne found the perfect home for the exotic plants he brought back from spells as Viceroy of India and Governor General of Canada. He created a subtropical paradise at Killmackillogue Bay, where rocks and hills tumble wildly to sheltered inlets and where the McFinnan Duffs once smuggled goods to and from Europe.

A century ago, Lord Lansdowne planted over 400 acres of woodland on the mountain acreage that had originally been granted to William Petty, Oliver Cromwell's surgeon, and which came into his family when Petty's daughter married Lord Kerry, later 1st Lord Lansdowne. The 5th Marquis spent 60 years creating the garden around the 19th-century house, introducing plants from all over the world: among them giant conifers, swamp cypress and redwoods from North America, tree ferns from the mountains of Australia, rhododendrons and hemlocks from China and Tibet, *Drimys winteri* and the

RIGHT A century ago, a subtropical paradise was created where the warm waters of the Gulf Stream meet this remote Kerry peninsula.

LEFT Rhododendrons grow to giant proportions, flourishing improbably beside the rocky shore of Killmackillogue Bay.

scarlet lanterned *Crinodendron hookerianum* from South America and the Japanese cypress *Cryptomeria japonica*. The result is a luxuriant garden of Eden where the contrast between the exotic primeval jungle of tree ferns, bamboos, towering conifers and brilliant rhododendrons and the glimpses of wild coast and mountain scenery set the senses reeling. Paths – each one a voyage into the unknown – wind through the moss and fern-carpeted woods and past natural outcrops of rock. Their names are evocative: King's Oozy, where Edward VII planted a tree in a squelchy spot; and the Knockatee Seat, a vantage point looking out over a sea of rosy *Rhododendron arboreum* towards the mountains. Lord Lansdowne personally supervised the collection of some of the rhododendrons from the Himalayas during his time India.

The best time to appreciate the collection in all its infinite variety is in April and May when the rhododendron display is at its height, although the season

LEFT *Some of the most fascinating effects in the garden are created by nature, as here with a stunning composition of bamboo, fallen leaves and mossy rock.*

RIGHT *The gardens were created by the 5th Marquis of Lansdowne as a foil to the 19th-century house, partially hidden by one of the huge outcrops of granite.*

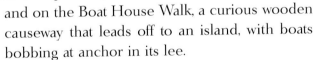

ABOVE Surrounded by wild mountain landscape, the isolated bay was once a favoured haunt of smugglers.

extends from as early as December to July. The blooms range from the perfumed pale pink trusses of *R.* 'Loderi King George' and the clear pink bells of *R.* Temple Belle Group to the nutmeg-scented, yellow-throated *R.* 'Frangrantissimum'. Stately large-leaved rhododendrons *R. falconeri* and *R. sinogrande* are represented, while at the other end of the scale is the dwarf *R. keiskei* with its lemon-yellow flowers.

Tree ferns, which come from the wet mountains of Australia, are perfectly at home in the damp Kerry climate and are a special feature at Derreen. Groves of them, spreading their six-feet fronds like umbrellas, stand as reminders of the plants of the primeval past. Autumn offers another display, as trees such as the *Parrotia persica* display shades of gold and vermillion and the swamp cypress *Taxodium distichum* turns a showy cinnamon. Seascapes come unexpectedly into view around the grounds and on the Boat House Walk, a curious wooden causeway that leads off to an island, with boats bobbing at anchor in its lee.

Derreen is still owned by descendants of the Lansdowne family: the estate passed to Lady Nairne, sister of the 7th Marquis, and is now owned by her son, the Hon. David Bigham. Planting continues at the estate under the supervision of Jacky Ward, whose father was head gardener before him. Derreen remains a wonderful example of the perfect marriage between Irish conditions and the principles expressed by William Robinson in his book, *The Wild Garden.*

LISSELAN

CLONAKILTY, COUNTY CORK

*An Edwardian garden, a haven for rhododendrons
and azaleas, with a romantic riverside setting.*

GARDENS IN IRELAND tend to occur in clumps, as though one wonderful garden inspired others. At Lisselan, ideas from the Robinsonian garden at Annes Grove (see page 104) took root on the banks of the river Argideen near Clonakilty. Here William Bence-Jones chose a site on a promontory above the river for a French chateau-style house, designed for him by Lewis Vulliamy in the early 1850s. William's successor, Reginald Bence-Jones, created 30 acres of gardens as a foil to the family's home, so that the stands of specimen trees and the turreted house are mirrored in a placid stretch of river.

The grounds are much as they were in their Edwardian heyday, with more formal areas near the house and a wild river garden, with rhododendrons predominating, laid out along the banks of the river. Among the features of that era are a shrubbery designed for seclusion and dalliance, a rockery – now planted with ericas, cistus and acers – and a pergola walk wreathed with roses. Other period details include a summer house thatched in heather and a walled garden which awaits restoration.

The layout of the garden makes full use of the natural slopes, resulting in flagged paths that wind along the side of the valley. There is a pool and fountain garden, next to which is an azalea garden. Among the many tender, rare plants that thrive in these grounds are tree ferns, acacia, eucalyptus and a Judas tree. The river, enhanced with weirs and bridges, affords a series of glorious vistas. At one point it has been widened to form a lake, complete with an island, and on the far bank a walk known as the Lady's Mile runs beside an old mill stream.

LEFT In Monet style, the lily pond reflects the blooming rhododendrons.

RIGHT Thirty acres of garden were created as a foil to the 1850s house.

ILNACULLIN

*An island paradise combining a wild garden crowned
with a formal jewel.*

ALL GARDENS are in a sense islands, small worlds where plants and fantasy float serenely and the gardener rules supreme. But Ilnacullin is that most magical thing of all: an island garden, embraced by the Gulf Stream and lying in the wooded arms of Glengarriff harbour. The 37 acres have been planted as a magical wild garden, with an enchanting Italian garden as the centrepiece.

In 1910 the rocky, gorse-covered island was bought from the War Office by Annan Bryce, who developed it as a garden, importing soil by the boatload and planting shelter belts. The central architectural features of the compartmentalised garden, designed for Bryce by English architect Harold Peto, are the wisteria-covered *casita* and the sunken Italian garden in classical Italian style, with its attendant pavilion. Here, the shapes of cypress, topiary and exotic shrubs accentuate the Mediterranean mood. The formality of a series of compartmentalised gardens with lawns, shrub borders and a kitchen garden with a magnificent double herbaceous border, contrast with the vistas of wild mountain and seascapes framed by special viewing points.

The Happy Valley, traversing the island from a Grecian temple, dipping to a bog garden and rising to a distant Martello tower, is the loveliest way to view rare shrubs and trees. There is also the aptly named Jungle, which is a perfect habitat for groves of unusual rhododendrons. In 1953 the garden was donated to the Irish nation and is now in the care of the Heritage Service. A visit here is a real adventure, with the added thrill of a voyage out to the island past the wooded shores of Glengarriff and Seal Island.

LEFT A stone carving with mythical creatures adds an exotic touch.

BELOW The island lies in a corner of Bantry Bay, sheltered in the wooded arms of Glengarriff Harbour.

LEFT The Pavilion and sunken Italian garden designed by Harold Peto were inspired by the courts of Pompeii and form one of the central features of the compartmentalised garden.

BELOW The clock tower, built to Harold Peto's design.

CREAGH

SKIBBEREEN, COUNTY CORK

A secret garden inspired by a painting where exotic plants flourish beside a sheltered inlet.

THERE ARE SOME gardens that seem to exert an influence beyond mere pleasure to the senses, and Creagh is one of them. The benign spell of this lovely wild garden, in the shelter of a wooded inlet, provided the inspiration for this book and its predecessors and also played a part in ensuring its own continuance for the enjoyment of future generations.

The garden was the creation of the late Peter and Gwendoline Harold-Barry, who bought the property in 1945. Around the pleasing bow-ended 1820 Regency house, with its existing sheltering and specimen trees, they laid out a garden which gave both the imagination and the advantages of the mild climate full reign. An old mill race and pond provided the opportunity for the most memorable part of the garden, which was inspired by a Rousseau painting. The banks of the serpentine pond are bound with a tapestry of green foliage plants, among which white-flowered calla lilies and roses glimmer in the dappled shade. The ruins of the old mill tower provide the perfect Gothic vista and the prospect towards the house is framed in an exotic jungle of large-leaved rhododendrons, palms and tree ferns.

This is a wild garden in the Robinsonian sense, where exotic and native plants grow together in happy profusion. Paths lead off to

RIGHT The doorway into the kitchen garden framed by rhododendrons comes to life in late spring, which is probably the best time of year to see the gardens.

RIGHT Purple sage, rosemary and lavender combine with box topiary in the walled garden.

mysterious destinations, a view of the seashore and Inisbeg Island framed in a wicket gate, a discreetly sited double seater lavatory where Victorian gentlemen used to go to smoke companionably and – rather more romantically – a 'proposal' bench overlooking the mill-pond. Other features to discover include the restored walled garden, where the poultry have palatial quarters known as the 'Hens' Hilton', a rose walk and many unusual shrubs and trees.

Like many elderly owners, the widowed Peter Harold-Barry was concerned for the future of his garden. Through a mutual interest in gardening, a fortuitous friendship was formed between Harold-Barry, Martin Sherry and Ken Lambert, culminating in the establishment of the Gwendoline Barry Trust, which gave both garden and owner a new lease of life. After Harold-Barry's death, his friends went on caring for the garden, keeping up the tradition and preserving the special atmosphere of this old world garden so that it continues to beguile visitors today.

RIGHT The thatched summer house, painted in a soft ochre, and suitably sited in a sheltered corner of the garden.

FAR RIGHT The wild garden around the serpentine mill pond was inspired by a painting by Rousseau. Overhanging trees and ferns are reflected in the still water.

T HE ORIGINAL NINE counties of Ulster combine the twin pleasures of variety and small-scale accessibility. To the east, the Ards Peninsula stretches a protective arm around the island-studded Strangford Lough; the mountains of Mourne shelter the sub-tropical niches on the northern shores of Carlingford Lough; and beyond the drumlins of County Down, Lough Neagh forms a moody inland sea. The north coast boasts the lovely Glens of Antrim, bracing cliffs and strands and the

A lichen-covered balustrade at Drenagh.

Carved stone creatures adorn the Dodo Terrace at Mount Stewart.

strong-backed hills of the Sperrins. The calm Lakelands of Fermanagh provide a complete contrast to the rugged beauty of Donegal, with scenery as wild as anything that Connemara or Kerry has to offer.

Among the compelling sights to be seen in this part of the country are the ruins of Dunluce Castle, perched perilously on a cliff edge in Antrim, and the Mussenden Temple, clinging vertiginously to the cliffs at Downhill, County Derry. There are also the majestic rocks of the Giant's Causeway, the fascinating waterscapes seen from the Erne waterways and the glorious strands of the Rosguill Peninsula in County Donegal.

There are sites of historical interest, too, such as Inch Abbey, a medieval monastery set amongst the marshes just outside Downpatrick in County Down, and in the

Sheep graze the cliff-tops at Downhill.

THE
NORTH

cathedral cemetery of Downpatrick itself, the grave of St Patrick. Then there is picturesque Glenarm, seat of the Earls of Antrim, the Norman castles, Elizabethan churches – the list of fascinating sights goes on. The Gulf Stream curls benignly around the coast so that northern gardens are lush, even sub-tropical, and their settings are stupendous.

Bishop Hervey's cenotaph, Downhill.

Set in idyllic surroundings, the gardens of the north include Glenveagh, with its colourful potager and imaginative informality, situated on a lake in a remote Donegal mountain valley; Mount Stewart, Ireland's premier garden on the Ards Peninsula; Rowallane in County Down, with its naturalistic Robinsonian garden and acre upon acre of magnificent flowering shrubs; and Drenagh, with its terraced Italianate grounds and secret white garden framed in a moon window.

MOUNT STEWART

*A series of beautifully conceived formal gardens
are the jewels in a matchless setting of woods,
water and glades.*

M OUNT STEWART, the grandest of all the gardens in the Six Counties, is deeply rewarding at every level. The formal structure of a series of brilliantly designed gardens forms the link between the architecture of the house and the wider setting of enchanting informal grounds laid out around a lake.

The formal gardens within the 19th-century ornamental estate were created by Edith, Lady Londonderry, and are especially memorable for her colourful planting and her whimsical symbolism. In one case, a flowery 'Red Hand of Ulster' is placed in front of a topiaried Celtic harp in the Shamrock garden. In a different scenario, family members feature atop the hedge in a fabled stag hunt retold in topiaried yew.

When the Londonderrys came to live at Mount Stewart in 1921, Lady Edith, known as 'Circe the Sorceress' to those in her powerful political coterie, thought it the dampest, darkest, saddest place to spend a winter.

While her husband took up the post of Minister for Education for Ulster, Edith poured her energies into establishing the gardens in only five years. She was aided in this endeavour by the mild climate breathed by the Gulf Stream, and by her knowledgeable gardening friends, Sir John Ross and

*LEFT The Jubilee Walk, marking
George V's Silver Jubilee, with a statue
of the legendary white stag.*

*FAR LEFT Bluebells carpet grass
beside the driveway, under a canopy
of spring foliage and blossom.*

ABOVE A detail of one of the stone creatures on the Dodo Terrace, carved by Thomas Beattie.

Sir Herbert Maxwell. Gertrude Jekyll is also said to have been consulted on the planting plan for the sunken garden. But Lady Edith devised her own brilliant lemon, orange, blue, and purple scheme for the four geometrical beds, with a surrounding raised terrace where delphiniums, hemerocallis and lilies form stars and spires against tree heath and azaleas, while clematis, wisteria and ceanothus festoon the pergola above golden iris.

In the Spanish garden, where the loggia looks out over a lawn with an oval pool at its centre, Lady Edith found the most original use for the dreaded *Cupressocyparis leylandii* – she had it clipped into airy arches. The cool green planting of hostas, glaucous, *Kniphofia caulescens* and hydrangeas is a complete contrast to the spicy palette of the Italian garden which runs the whole width of the house. The design of geometric beds, where one side of the garden is filled with hot colours and the other with cooler tones, each laid out around a central fountain, was inspired by her childhood home at Dunrobin Castle.

Each parterre has a different colour scheme and co-ordinating hedge: ruby cotinus with clamouring purple, and the scarlets and oranges of golden privet with fiery *Crocosmia* 'Lucifer' and *Dahlia* 'Bishop of Llandaff' in another section. Under the dappled shade of eucalyptus, pale beauties like *Campanula lactiflora* 'Loddon Anna', *Phlox paniculata* 'Norah Leigh' and *Nepeta govaniana* are used. The terrace and stone work were inspired by Villa Gamberaia and the Villa Farnese, the architectural detail offset with brilliant pink *Salvia involucrata*, crinum lilies and *Beschorneria yuccoides*.

Most romantic of all the gardens is the enclosed Mairi garden, named after the Londonderrys' youngest daughter. She was born after the couple were reconciled following the ending of a long-

ABOVE A curious inhabitant of the Noah's Ark on the Dodo Terrace.

running affair by Lady Edith's husband, who was known as 'Charlie the Cheetah' after one of the stone creatures on the nearby Dodo Terrace. Lady Edith was a powerful political hostess and other creatures on the impressive Terrace represent the members of the exclusive 'Ark Club', among them Winston (Churchill) the Warlock and Harold (Macmillan) the Humming Bird, who would be flown into Mount Stewart for restorative weekends. The wonderfully imaginative stonework was carved by local man Thomas Beattie.

The circular garden echoes the theme of the popular nursery rhyme with silver bells of campanulas and a central fountain surrounded by cockle shells amid drifts of silver, blue and white plants, with hydrangeas and agapanthus providing the most vivid blues of all. White fantail doves strut and coo beside the stone summer house.

A walk through the further reaches of the demesne meanders through the lily wood, around the lake and up to the mysterious towers of Tir Na Nog (Land of the Ever Young) where the Londonderry family are buried.

ABOVE Leyland cypresses have been clipped into tall arches in the Spanish garden.

LEFT In the Shamrock garden, the Red Hand of Ulster features beside the Celtic Harp.

RIGHT A huge cloud of Olearia rani, a splendid sight in the lengthening days of spring, almost hides a stone bench in the Mairi garden.

ABOVE Swans preen by the lake, with the towers of Tir Na Nog behind.

Here, the gazebos were built by another local man, Joe Girvan, their fantastical shapes offset by the brilliant foliage of Japanese maples, silvery olive trees (seeded from the Mount of Olives), and feathery *Cupressus cashmeriana*. Also not to be missed is the exquisite classical folly on the shores of the Lough known as the Temple of the Winds, designed as a banqueting house by James 'Athenian' Stewart for the 1st Marquis of Londonderry.

Each of the walks in the garden has its own mood. In the shade of the Lily wood, scented rhododendrons and azaleas are interspersed with showy lilies, statuesque *Cardiocrinum giganteum, Lilium monadelphum L.* 'Shuksan' and pink and white *L. martagon*. The Ladies walk – an original path used for constitutionals – and the Rhododendron Hill feature some of the largest and oldest rhododendrons on the estate. The lakeside Rock walk gets its name from the rocky outcrop around which it winds. Japanese maples, lacquer-red rhododendrons and a pagoda

LEFT Hydrangeas and waterlilies abound around the margins of the lake.

ABOVE Ferns unfurl spring fronds beside the lake walk. The path is lined with rare trees and flowering shrubs.

gives this walk an oriental feel. The Lake walk, brilliant with colour in spring and autumn, works its own tranquil magic as water fowl draw silver arrows across the reflection of Tir Na Nog's fairytale towers. When Lady Edith began creating the gardens she wondered if they would ever rival the luxuriance of the sub-tropical gardens of Devon and Cornwall. Eighty years later, the gardens – now maintained by the National Trust and by the head gardener Nigel Marshall – provide their own answer.

GLENVEAGH

CHURCHILL, COUNTY DONEGAL

*A garden which combines the formal
and informal with wonderful planting and a
superbly majestic location.*

GLENVEAGH CASTLE and gardens are located in a starkly beautiful setting beside Lough Veagh in the isolated mountain splendour of Glenveagh National Park. In the midst of the desolate moorland surroundings, the luxuriance of the gardens, where palms and frost-tender plants flourish, seem all the more exotic. Formal terraces and walks traverse wild gardens lush with damp-loving plants. Behind the castle is a walled garden in high Victorian style where prolific herbaceous borders compete with neat ranks of colourful vegetables.

The baronial granite castle was completed in 1873 for John George Adair, who made his fortune speculating in estates bankrupted by the Famine. A litigious character, Adair became infamous for clearing Glenveagh of tenants, in the last mass eviction to take place in Ireland. He was outlived by the rich American widow he had married, Cornelia Ritchie, and under her care Glenveagh embarked on a happier chapter of its history. Shelter belts were planted and a potager and pleasure ground laid out.

The present lovely incarnation of the gardens began after the end of the second World War, when American art expert Henry McIlhenny returned to the castle and started to transform the neglected grounds. He was helped in this task by his Harvard classmate and landscape designer Lanning Roper and English gardener James Russell. McIlhenny disliked seeing bare earth and planted the pleasure grounds with green rivers of foliage plants such as

*ABOVE Lichens flourish
on a stem of a tree in the
pure Donegal air.*

*RIGHT A sea of foliage
plants swirls beneath tree
ferns and rhododendrons.*

gunneras, *Dicksonia antarctica*, rodgersias, phormium, hostas, ferns and astilbes, interspersed with rare rhododendrons and flowering shrubs. Not wanting a garden which 'began anywhere and ended nowhere', McIlhenny added a strong structural framework affording vistas and vantage points. He lined the Swiss walk with azaleas, filled the Italian garden with classical statues and created the 'Stairway to the Stars' which rises 67 steps to afford spectacular views of the lake.

The Belgian walk, created by convalescing Belgian soldiers during the first World War, was embellished with terracotta pots and statues. Formality, straight lines and economy of design were used to give a sense of relief and order from the wonderful chaos of natural planting. However, in the Pleasure Ground, the natural profusion was made still more exotic with the addition of subtropical plants such as palms, tree ferns and stately shrubs like the

BELOW The gothic conservatory in the kitchen garden was designed by Philippe Julian and looks out over the colourful potager.

ABOVE *A lead cherub is half hidden by riotous blooms of hemerocallis in the walled garden.*

large-leaved rhododendrons. The potager was Henry McIlhenny's particular pride and joy, for he loved flowers and would arrange 76 vasefuls a week for his house guests. Around the stone walls and on either side of the central walk are deep herbaceous borders burgeoning with monkshood, goat's rue, phlox, black-eyed *Geranium* 'Ann Folkard', the lilies that McIlhenny loved and all manner of handsome plants. White flowers and variegated plants were also a particular favourite of his, for he believed that they relieved the 'Irish greenness'.

In the centre of the garden, decorative vegetables, such as ruby chard, leeks and salad onions parade behind immaculately clipped curlicues and hedges of box. In one corner of the garden is a picturesque thatched gardener's cottage, which could have come straight from the pages of a Beatrix Potter tale, while a Gothic conservatory designed by Philippe Julian adds an altogether grander note. There are many noteworthy plants – *Michelia doltsopa*, *Rhododendron cinnabarinum* and *R. falconeri*, *Metrosideros lucidus* among them – in what is a beautifully maintained garden for all seasons. The gardens are all the more spectacular for their setting in completely unspoilt lake and mountain scenery.

RIGHT Antique Italian statuary and terracotta pots from the Imprunetta Pottery in Florence. The display is enhanced in spring with the blooms of camellias and rhododendrons.

LEFT Tree ferns, large-leaved rhododendrons, and foliage plants like hostas and gunneras add to the palette of greens in the pleasure grounds.

ABOVE Stewartia koreana underplanted with ferns (Blechnum cordatum) provides a verdant show.

In 1975, Henry McIlhenny sold the lands at Glenveagh to the government to ensure their conservation as a national park. In 1983, in keeping with his own beliefs, the castle and its grounds passed from private to public ownership. McIlhenny donated them to the nation so that the entire estate would remain a wonderful entity. The castle and gardens are at the heart of the wild and rugged Glenveagh National Park and the most colourful displays can be seen from May to August. The gardens also play an important role in educating local school children in environmental conservations. Visitors to Glenveagh must park at the interpretative centre and travel to the estate by shuttle bus so that the peace of the gardens remains undisturbed.

DOWNHILL CASTLE

*A spectacular temple, a water meadow and wonderful
follies are the main features of this demesne.*

I F EVER THERE WAS a fitting monument to one of the great eccentrics of the Georgian era it is the Mussenden Temple. Sublimely situated on the edge of a rocky cliff, 200 feet above Magilligan Strand, the temple was built for the worldly Earl of Bristol and Bishop of Derry, Frederick Augustus Hervey, by his adopted son and collaborator in his multifarious building schemes, architect Michael Shanahan. Some indication of the wealthy bishop's lifestyle may be gathered from the fact that he travelled so extravagantly in Europe that the chain of Bristol Hotels were named after him.

The temple is dedicated to the object of his scandalous admiration, his cousin Mrs Frideswide Mussenden, a great beauty of her day who died at the age of 22 before its completion. Designed as a library, the temple, inspired by the Temple of Vesta at Tivoli,

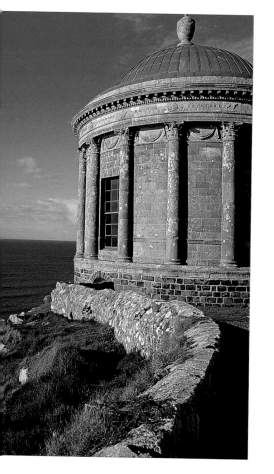

LEFT The spectacularly sited Mussenden Temple, built on a cliff edge for the worldly bishop of Derry, Frederick Augustus Hervey.

BELOW The ruins of Downhill Castle – one of the palaces of the eccentric Earl Bishop of Derry.

Rome, was completed in 1785 and adorned the demesne surrounding 1770s
Downhill Castle, just one of the bishop's three palatial homes. The temple is
just one of the follies in the grounds of the castle, which is now in spectacular
ruins following partial demolition in the 1950s. At the entrance is a Roman triumphal arch with an entrancing gate lodge at its flank. Known appropriately as
the Bishop's Gate, it was built in 1784, probably by Shanahan. For decades the
lodge was the home of National Trust warden Jan Eccles, who gardened well
into her 90s and created the colourful water meadow and flower garden
beyond the Bishop's Gate as well as planting many notable trees. The water
garden is glorious with violet *Iris kaempferi* and varicoloured Candelabra primulas in early summer. There is also a romantic garden with herbaceous borders
full of old-fashioned favourites and a pergola draped with scented roses.

The Bishop's enthusiasm for building projects also extended to the
grandiose Lion Gate, a canine palace in the form of a temple designed by John
Soane. The Gate was a cenotaph to the memory of his brother based on the
tomb of the Julii. A circular castellated gazebo in the Black Glen, known as
Lady Erne's seat, was also installed in honour of the Bishop's daughter.

ROWALLANE

*One of Ireland's foremost wild gardens, planted
amid rocks in a natural paradise.*

IN APRIL, May and June, a vast display of pink, mauve and purple rhododendrons and azaleas known as 'Wilson's Best Fifty' greets visitors to the aptly named Spring Ground at Rowallane. The planting is a glorious illustration of the genius of Hugh Armitage Moore, who, in the great shoulders of whinstone rock shrugging through the thin, acid pastures of his farm, saw the opportunity to create a wonderful garden in the Robinsonian manner. He also took the chance to incorporate the latest introductions from the great plant collectors like E. H. Wilson and Frank Kingdon Ward.

The result is a paradise set in 52 acres of wild flower meadows, woodland and natural rock garden, which is planted with rare trees, shrubs and rounded off by the splendid rhododendron collection. If the place breathes its own peaceful balm to the soul, perhaps it is because of the harmony between carefully sited plants and ideal, natural surroundings. At the heart of the estate is the old walled garden built by Hugh's uncle, the Reverend John Moore, who began planting the grounds and had the unusual stone cairns built from rounded river stones.

The walled garden is full of inspirational ideas, both in terms of covetable plants, like the handsome *Crinum* x *powellii*, and unusual associations, such as brilliant scarlet *Euphorbia* 'Fireglow' and handsome *E. characias wulfenii* cheek by jowl with blood-red *Rosa moyesii*. The walled garden is also home to the national penstemon collection – with more than 50 varieties represented – and

LEFT An urn acts as a finial above the gateway of the walled garden.

RIGHT The outer walled garden provides shelter for rare shrubs, while classical urns add a touch of grandeur to a small pool.

BELOW Formed by natural outcrops of whinstone, the Rock garden provides a perfect habitat for ericas, ferns and alpine plants.

rare climbing shrubs and herbaceous plants flourish within its shelter. An attractive yellow, blue and silver planting scheme, where an old pump backed with a circle of yew is draped in *Tropaeoleum speciosum* and set off by massed summer planting of hostas, *Kirengeshoma palmata* and deep blue agapanthus and displays of colchicums, meconopsis and primulas, are among the attractions.

The wild garden was created by Hugh Armitage Moore after he inherited the property in 1903. Paths mown through meadow and drystone walls with no fewer than 38 gates delineate the way through the different areas. Each has its own special atmosphere. 'The Hospital' (once used for sick calves) has a collection of unusual trees including the magnificent handkerchief tree, *Davidia involucrata*. The Rock garden has been planted with a collection of ericas, dwarf conifers, alpines and primulas including *P.* 'Rowallane Rose', the garden's own cultivar. The Bishop's rock takes it name from a throne-shaped outcrop with a stream planted with *Gunnera manicata*, *Primula florindae*, hostas and astilbes.

In the Pleasure Ground, the meadows surrounding the pond and 1860 bandstand are dotted with orchids and naturalised fritillaries in season. Among the cultivars that originated in the garden are *Hypericum* 'Rowallane' and the quince, *Chaenomeles*

ABOVE Fothergilla
'Monticola Group' and
azaleas flame into a
blaze of autumn scarlet
and gold – a final
flourish before the long
days of winter.

LEFT The berries of
mountain rowan
gleam scarlet among
the evergreens.

superba 'Rowallane'. The peak time for the wild garden is in May and June when the rhododendron display is at its height – but it is still lovely at any time. August is starred with the white flowers of eucryphias and hoherias and the 'snow' from seeding *Populus maximowiczii*. In September the wide variety of acers and viburnums begin to turn gold and crimson, and in the Paddock, Mediterranean and southern hemisphere shrubs provide interest from spring to autumn.

DRENAGH

LIMAVADY, COUNTY DERRY

*A moon garden and classical and
Robinsonian gardening traditions are all represented
in a 300-year-old estate.*

THIS FINE ESTATE reflects a multi-generational history stretching back 300 years. The words of John Seddon, in *Garden Craft Old and New* in 1890 were never more true than for Drenagh: 'In the case of an old garden, mellowed by time, we have to note something that goes beyond mere surface beauty. The old ground embodies bygone conceptions of ideal beauty: it has absorbed human thoughts and memories.'

The Georgian love affair with classicism, the wild gardening tradition and the romantic gardening style are all represented here. The latter is memorably encapsulated in the Moon garden, filled with the pale elegance of white-flowered and silver-leaved plants and named for the Chinese-style circular window framing a view of an arboretum, luxuriant in a myriad shades of green. The curious wall niches in the Moon garden are also reminders of the past: these are 'bee boles', or shelters for straw bee skeps.

The McCausland family first came to the estate in the 1680s, when Robert McCausland married Hannah, daughter of the 'Speaker' Conolly of Castletown House and the property

LEFT The classical fountain, which is dramatically sited at the foot of an escarpment, was inspired by a Florentine counterpart at the Villa d'Este.

RIGHT The curious bee boles, where bee skeps were kept during the winter, framed in the Moon Window, which forms the entrance to the Moon garden.

was bequeathed to him. Further advantageous marriages followed, and the McCauslands engaged in the Georgian passion for building. The first was a house known as Fruithill, of which the Gothic gate lodge is a reminder. Robert's great, great grandson Marcus commissioned Charles Lanyon to build a classical mansion (the architect's first major commission), for his heiress wife Marianne Tyndall, and this was completed in 1837.

The terraced gardens in the Italian style and the dramatic fountain, inspired by a design at the Villa d'Este and sited at the foot of an escarpment, all date from this period. So, too, do the arboretum and the pleasure grounds. The

BELOW The Italianate terraces are contemporary with the 1837 classical mansion. The stone balustrade provides a romantic vantage point over the surrounding gardens and countryside.

ABOVE The arboretum is luxuriant with myriad shades of green, and carpeted with bluebells in the spring.

ABOVE RIGHT Skunk cabbage (Lysichiton americanus) lines the stream running through the glen.

enthusiasm for wild Robinsonian planting and for new species discovered by plant hunters is reflected in the streamside garden, and in the hybrid rhododendrons planted in the area known as the Glen. Major additions were made to the garden in the 1960s, following the designs of the Canadian landscape artist Frances Rhoades and incorporating the Moon garden, an English garden and an azalea garden.

Now Conolly McCausland, with his wife Sheelagh, is continuing the restoration work begun by his parents. The old orchard which gave the first house its name is to be cleared, the Moon garden is to be replanted with silver and white-flowered plants like phlox, *Romneya coulteri*, lilies, Japanese anemones and artemisia, so that the plants in each half mirror each other. The greenhouses in the walled garden are also being restored in keeping with the Victorian kitchen garden tradition. Together, Lanyon's classical Georgian house – which marks the transition to his later Victorian style – and the 300-year-old history of the grounds, offer a fascinating insight into changing tastes.

WHERE TO VISIT

Annes Grove, p104
CASTLETOWNROCHE,
COUNTY CORK
OPEN Mon-Sat, 10am-5pm;
Sunday 1-6pm, from March 16
to Sep 30. Other times by
appointment.
Tel & fax: +353 22 26145
DIRECTIONS Annes Grove is
1.6km north of Castletownroche
on the Fermoy Road.

Ballinlough Castle, p94
CLONMELLON, COUNTY
WESTMEATH
OPEN Tues, Wed, Thur, Sat and
bank holidays from 11am-6pm,
Sun from 2-6pm, from May 1 to
September 30. Other times by
arrangement.
Tel: +353 46 33135
Fax: +353 46 33331
DIRECTIONS Ballinlough is
on the N52 between Kells and
Mullingar, signposted from
Athboy.

Ballymaloe, p109
COOKERY SCHOOL GARDENS,
SHANAGARRY, COUNTY CORK
OPEN Daily, 9am-6pm from
April to October.
Tel: +353 21 646785
Fax +353 21 646909
DIRECTIONS Turn off the main
Cork-Waterford Road (N25) at
Castlemartyr and follow signs to
the Cookery School on the
Shanagarry Road (632).

Birr Castle, p74
BIRR, COUNTY OFFALY
OPEN Daily, 9am-6pm, all year.
Tel +353 509 20336
Fax: +353 509 21583
DIRECTIONS Located in Birr centre.

Butterstream, p80
TRIM, COUNTY MEATH
OPEN Daily, 11am-6pm, from
April to September. Groups any
time by appointment. Teas served
and plants for sale.

Tel: +353 46 36017.
Fax: +353 46 31702
DIRECTIONS Signposted from the
outskirts of Trim, Butterstream is
about 40 minutes' drive from
Dublin.

Camas Park, p16
CASHEL, COUNTY TIPPERARY
OPEN By appointment to groups.
Tel: +353 62 61010
DIRECTIONS Turn right at the
junction at the south end of
Cashel. Camas Park is 3km fur-
ther on, to the left.

Creagh, p124
SKIBBEREEN, COUNTY CORK
OPEN Daily, 10am-6pm, from
March 1 to October 31. Other
times by appointment.
Tel & fax: +353 28 22121
DIRECTIONS Look out for signs
on the Skibbereen to Baltimore
Road (N595), a few km from
Baltimore.

Derreen, p114
KENMARE, COUNTY KERRY
OPEN Daily, 10am-6pm, from
April 1 to September 31.
Telephone: +353 64 83103
DIRECTIONS Derreen is off the
Kenmare-Castletownbere Road
(R571), just outside Lauragh.

The Dillon Garden, p48
45 SANDFORD ROAD, DUBLIN
OPEN Daily, 2-6pm, in March
July and August; Sundays only,
2-6pm in April, May, June and
September.
Tel & fax: +353 1 4971308.
DIRECTIONS In a cul-de-sac just
off Sandford Road, turn right at
the Merton Road church.

Downhill Castle, p14
COLERAINE, COUNTY DERRY
OPEN Daily from dawn until dusk.
The temple is open at weekends,
2pm-6pm, from Easter to
October (daily in high summer).

Tel & fax:: 01265 848728
DIRECTIONS Downhill is at
Portstewart Strand, not far
from Coleraine.

Drenagh, p152
LIMAVADY, COUNTY DERRY
OPEN To groups by appointment.
Tel: 01504 722649
Fax: 01504 722061
DIRECTIONS Drenagh is 1.6km
from Limavady on the Coleraine
Road.

Emo Court, p84
EMO, COUNTY LAOIS
OPEN Daily in daylight hours.
Tel: +353 502 26573
DIRECTIONS Emo is on the R422
off the Dublin-Cork N7 between
Monasterevin and Portlaoise.

Fairfield Lodge, p58
MONKSTOWN AVENUE,
COUNTY DUBLIN
OPEN Sun, Wed and bank holi-
days, 2-6pm from May-
September. Telephone: +353 1
2803912
DIRECTIONS Fairfield Lodge is
near the top of Monkstown
Avenue on the left-hand side.

Glenveagh, p138
CHURCHILL, COUNTY DONEGAL
OPEN Daily, 10am-6.30pm, from
Easter to 1st Sun in November.
Closed Fridays in October and
November.
Tel: +353 74 37090
Fax: +353 74 37072
DIRECTIONS Glenveagh is 13km
from Churchill on the R251.

Ilnacullin, p122
GARNISH ISLAND, GLENGARRIFF,
COUNTY CORK
OPEN Mon-Sat from 10am-
4.30pm, and Sun 10am-4.30pm
in April, May, June and
September; Mon- Sat from
10am-6.30pm, Sun 1-7pm in
July and August; Mon-Sat from

9.30am-6.30pm , Sun 11am-
7pm in March and October.
DIRECTIONS Departures by boat
from Glengarriff. Landings one
hour before closing time.

Johnstown Castle, p24
MURRINTOWN, COUNTY
WEXFORD
OPEN Daily, 9.am-5pm.
Telephone: +353 53 42888
DIRECTIONS From Wexford, take
the Rosslare Road. Johnstown is
signposted from the first turning
on the right.

Kilfane, p12
THOMASTOWN, COUNTY
KILKENNY
OPEN Sun only, 2-6pm from
September to April. Daily 11am-
6pm in July and August.
Tel: +353 56 24558
Fax: +353 56 27491
e-mail: www.NicholasMosse.com
DIRECTIONS the turning for
Kilfane is 3km outside
Thomastown on the Dublin-
Waterford Road.

Kilmokea, p20
CAMPILE, COUNTY WEXFORD
OPEN Daily, 10am-5pm from
April to November.
Tel: +353 51 388109
Fax: +353 51 388776
DIRECTIONS Take the R733 from
New Ross past the JFK
Arboretum, turn right for Great
Island, the garden is 1.5km down
the road, on the right.

Killruddery, p60
BRAY, COUNTY WICKLOW
OPEN Daily, 1-5pm, from April to
September. Groups by appointment at other times.
Tel & fax +353 1 2862777
DIRECTIONS Killruddery is 2km
south of Bray. Take the third exit
from N11, travelling south, and
follow signs from the round-
about.

Knockcree, *p68*
CARRICKMINES, COUNTY DUBLIN
OPEN Sundays, 2-6pm, April-July
and by appointment to groups.
Tel: + 353 1 2955884
DIRECTIONS Knockcree is south
west of Foxrock village, one third
the way up the Glenamuck Road
towards Enniskerry.

Larchill, *p90*
KILCOCK, COUNTY KILDARE
OPEN Daily, 12-6pm, from May
to September.
Tel 8 fax:: +353 1 6284580
DIRECTIONS Take the second
Kilcock exit coming from
Dublin, then take the
Summerhill – Trim Road, turn
right at the sign for Larchill and
keep following the signs.

Lisselan, *p121*
CLONAKILTY, COUNTY CORK
OPEN Daily, 9am-7pm, from
March to October, or to groups
by appointment.
Tel: +353 23 33249
Fax: +353 23 34605
DIRECTIONS Lisselan is on the
main Cork-Clonakilty Road
(N71), signposted from just
beyond Ballinascorthy.

Lodge Park, *p32*
STRAFFAN, COUNTY KILDARE
OPEN Tuesday-Friday and
Sundays, from 2.-6pm in June
and July, and Tuesday-Friday
from 2.30-5.30pm in August.
Other times by appointment.
Tel: +353 1 6273155
/6288412
Fax: +353 1 6273477.
DIRECTIONS Follow signposts for
'Steam Museum' just outside
Straffan. Turn off the N4 at
Lucan or Maynooth, or off the
N7 at Kill.

Mount Stewart, *p130*
NEWTOWNARDS, COUNTY DOWN
OPEN Daily (except Tuesdays), 1-
6pm, from April to September.
Tel: 012477 88387/88487
Fax: 012477 88569
DIRECTIONS Mount Stewart is on

the east shore of Strangford
Lough, 8km from Newtownards
on the A20 to Portaferry.

Mount Usher, *p96*
ASHFORD, COUNTY WICKLOW
OPEN Daily, from 10.30am-6pm,
from early March to October 31.
Tel:+353 404 40116
Fax: +353 404 40205
DIRECTIONS On the N11 Dublin
to Wexford Road on the south
side of Ashford.

Powerscourt, *p42*
ENNISKERRY, COUNTY WICKLOW
OPEN Daily, 9.30am-5.30pm.
Winter opening times are
subject to alteration.
Tel: +353 1 204 6000
Fax: +353 1 286 3561
DIRECTIONS Powerscourt is sign-
posted from the N11 south of
Bray.

Ram House, *p28*
COOLGREANY, COUNTY WEXFORD
OPEN Fri, Sat, Sun and bank holi-
days, from 2.30-6pm in May,
June, July and August and to
groups by appointment.
Tel 8 fax: +353 402 37238
DIRECTIONS On the N11 between
Arklow and Gorey, take the turn
for Coolgreaney at Inch post
office. Ram House is on the edge
of the village.

Rathmichael Lodge, *p54*
RATHMICHAEL, COUNTY DUBLIN
OPEN By appointment only from
mid-May to end July.
Tel: +353 1 2822203
DIRECTIONS Leave the N11 for
Shankill at Loughlinstown, at the
start of the Bray bypass, take the
first right at petrol station, turn
sharp left into Ballybride Road at
church gate. Rathmichael Lodge
is the third on the right.

Rowallane, *p146*
SAINTFIELD, COUNTY DOWN
OPEN Mon-Fri 10.30am-6pm, Sat
and Sun 2-6pm from April to
October. Mon-Fri 10.30am-5pm
from November to end March.

Tel: 01238 510131.
DIRECTIONS Rowallane is just out-
side Saintfield on the A7 Belfast-
Downpatrick Road.

Strokestown Park, *p99*
STROKESTOWN, COUNTY
ROSCOMMON
OPEN 11am-5.30pm, from April
to October. Restaurant facilities
available.

Tel: +353 78 33013
Fax: +353 78 33712.
e-mail: info@strokestownpark.ie
DIRECTIONS Strokestown Park is
in the middle of Strokestown on
the Dublin-Sligo N5.

INDEX

ACKNOWLEDGEMENTS

Marianne Heron would like to thank all the
garden owners featured in this book and everyone who assisted in
the research for sharing their own special havens and their
knowledge with such unfailing enthusiasm.

Steven Wooster would also like to thank all the garden owners, in
particular for their hospitality in providing tea, coffee and sometimes
something a little stronger – much needed in the cold, grey and
windy days of the Irish summer. He is also grateful to John from the
mobile fish and chip van at Glengarriff for taking him to Ilnacullin on
the 'Harbour Queen' ferry.

The publishers would like to thank the National Trust and Dúchas –
the Heritage Service – for allowing their gardens to be
photographed; Sorcha Hitchcox for her editorial assistance, David
Fordham and Christine Wood for their work on the initial design
concept, and Marie Lorimer for compiling the index.

The boat house at Creagh